A Winter Magic Tour Through Holiday Cookies

Whisking Up Winter Magic: Introduction to Holiday Cookies

Nathan Harper

Table of Contents

INTRODUCTION 6

CHAPTER I: The Magic of Winter Ingredients 8

Highlighting key seasonal ingredients 8

Tips for selecting quality ingredients 11

Emphasizing the flavors of winter 14

CHAPTER II: Essential Baking Tools and Techniques 18

Overview of necessary tools 18

Basic baking techniques 21

Tips for success in holiday cookie baking 25

CHAPTER III: Classic Holiday Cookie Recipes 29

Sugar cookies with festive decorations 29

Gingerbread cookies with royal icing 32

Peppermint chocolate chip cookies 36

CHAPTER IV: Creative Twists on Tradition 40

Cranberry orange shortbread cookies........................ 40

Pistachio and cardamom snowballs 43

Chocolate-dipped almond biscotti 47

Chapter V: International Flavors 51

German Lebkuchen 51

Italian pizzelle 54

French sablés 57

Chapter VI: Gluten-Free and Vegan Options **61**

Almond flour snowball cookies 61

Vegan gingerbread men 64

Gluten-free peppermint brownie bites 68

CHAPTER VII: Gift-Worthy Treats **72**

Packaging ideas for holiday cookies 72

Tips for shipping cookies 75

Creating cookie gift baskets 78

CHAPTER VIII: Cookie Decorating Techniques **82**

Royal icing basics 82

Piping and flooding techniques 85

Edible glitter and embellishments 89

CHAPTER IX: Hosting a Cookie Swap **94**

Planning and organizing a cookie swap 94

Recipes for a successful event 98

Tips for a memorable gathering 101

CHAPTER X: Holiday Cookie Traditions Around the World
.... **105**

Exploring global holiday cookie customs 105

Learning about unique regional recipes 107

Incorporating diverse flavors into your holiday baking 110

CHAPTER XI: Preserving Winter Magic **114**

Storing Cookies for Freshness 114

Tips for Freezing and Shipping Holiday Treats 117

CONCLUSION **121**

INTRODUCTION

This is "A Winter Magic Tour Through Holiday Cookies: Whisking Up Winter Magic – Introduction to Holiday Cookies." When the earth is covered in a sparkling layer of frost throughout the winter, there's no better way to enjoy the magic of the holidays than by engaging in the beautiful craft of cookie baking. In this heartwarming journey, we invite you to embark on a culinary adventure that transcends the ordinary, whisking up a symphony of flavors and aromas that define the magic of winter.

This e-book celebrates tradition, inventiveness, and the wonderful atmosphere of holiday baking—it's much more than just a compilation of recipes. You'll learn the techniques for making a stunning variety of cookies that perfectly reflect the spirit of the occasion as we turn the pages together. From timeless classics like sugar cookies adorned with festive decorations to innovative twists on traditional recipes, we'll explore diverse flavors reflecting winter's warmth and magic.

In the ensuing chapters, we'll dive into the core of holiday cookie baking, including tips and tricks for essential ingredients, equipment, and methods to empower bakers of all skill levels. Whether you're passionate about perfecting the art of cookie decoration, interested in international cookie traditions, or seeking gluten-free and vegan options, this e-book has something for everyone.

Beyond the kitchen, we'll guide you in hosting memorable cookie swaps, creating personalized cookie gift baskets, and even inspiring you to document your winter magic with a personalized cookbook. Join us as we explore the joy of baking, sharing, and savoring moments that make the holiday season unique.

So, grab your apron, preheat your oven, and embark on a Winter Magic Tour Through Holiday Cookies – a journey that promises to fill your home with the sweet aroma of joy and create lasting memories with every baked batch.

CHAPTER I

The Magic of Winter Ingredients

Highlighting key seasonal ingredients

The season's essence is the magic of holiday baking, created by the essential seasonal ingredients that turn everyday recipes into delightful treats. As winter blankets the world in a chilly embrace, the pantry undergoes a seasonal shift, welcoming an array of ingredients that capture the essence of the holidays. Chief among these is the triumphant return of spices, and it's the aromatic trio of cinnamon, nutmeg, and cloves sets the stage for a symphony of flavors. These warm and comforting spices infuse holiday cookies with a nostalgic aroma, evoking memories of crackling fires and family gatherings. Cinnamon, in particular, takes center stage, adding a sweet and earthy note that pairs seamlessly with the rich, buttery undertones of many holiday treats.

Beyond spices, the winter season introduces an array of fresh and dried fruits that lend sweetness and tartness to holiday cookies. Cranberries burst onto the scene with their vibrant red hue, providing a pop of color and a tangy kick that balances the sweetness of doughs and icings. Marrying cranberries with orange zest creates a dynamic flavor profile, a pairing that has become a hallmark of holiday baking. Similarly, dried fruits such as apricots, figs, and dates offer a chewy texture and concentrated sweetness, elevating the complexity of cookie recipes.

In their various forms, nuts also play a starring role in holiday baking. Almonds, walnuts, and pecans bring a satisfying crunch while imparting their rich, nutty essence to cookies. Whether finely ground to fortify cookie bases or coarsely chopped to add texture, nuts contribute depth and character, making each bite a sensory experience. Toasting these nuts before incorporating them into recipes intensifies their flavor, creating a warm and toasty undertone that complements the winter theme.

As the temperature drops, the produce section welcomes a parade of citrus fruits, injecting a burst of sunshine into winter recipes. Oranges, lemons, and limes add a zesty brightness that cuts through the richness of butter and sugar, providing balance and a refreshing contrast. Citrus zest becomes a secret weapon with its concentrated aromatic oils, infusing baked goods with a burst of citrusy essence without excess moisture that can compromise texture.

Butter, that indulgent cornerstone of baking, takes on a special significance during the holiday season. Its rich, creamy flavor imparts a luxurious quality to cookies, creating a melt-in-your-mouth texture that defines classic holiday treats. Unsalted butter is preferred, allowing bakers to control the salt content and ensuring a pure, clean taste that enhances the overall flavor profile.

The sweeteners of choice also undergo a seasonal shift, with brown sugar and molasses taking center stage. Brown sugar, with its molasses content, adds depth and moisture to cookie dough, contributing to a chewy and tender texture. Molasses, derived from sugar cane or sugar beets, not only sweetens but imparts a distinct richness and a hint of caramel undertones. These darker sweeteners align with the cozy, comforting ambiance of the season, infusing cookies with a warmth that resonates with holiday traditions.

Flour, the backbone of many baked goods, undergoes subtle variations in holiday recipes. All-purpose flour forms the base, but adding ingredients like ground oats or almond flour introduces unique textures and flavors. These alternative flours not only cater to dietary preferences but also contribute to the overall complexity of the cookie.

The dairy aisle, too, embraces the spirit of the season, with eggs and dairy products playing essential roles in achieving the desired texture and structure of holiday cookies. Eggs provide leavening and moisture, contributing to the softness and rise of the final product. Milk, cream, or yogurt may be added for richness, ensuring each bite is a decadent indulgence.

In the realm of extracts, vanilla takes precedence; its

sweet and floral notes complement the array of flavors in holiday cookies. Pure vanilla extract, with its concentrated flavor derived from vanilla beans, adds a sophisticated depth that enhances the overall taste profile. For those seeking a more festive twist, almond and peppermint extracts make cameo appearances, infusing cookies with distinct and evocative essences.

Beyond individual ingredients, the magic of holiday

baking lies in the alchemy of their combinations. The careful balance of sweet and tart, the interplay of spices and herbs, and the layering of textures transform a mixture of ingredients into a sensory experience as winter's magic unfolds in the kitchen; incorporating these vital seasonal ingredients becomes a ritual, a way to infuse each cookie with the spirit of the season.

In conclusion, the allure of holiday cookies lies in baking

and the careful selection and harmonious blending of vital seasonal ingredients. These elements, each chosen for its unique contribution, create a tapestry of flavors and aromas embodying winter's magic. As you embark on your winter magic tour through holiday cookies, savor the journey of exploring and experimenting with these ingredients, letting the season's warmth unfold in every delectable bite.

Tips for selecting quality ingredients

The art of baking transcends the mere combination of ingredients; it hinges on the meticulous selection of high-quality components that lay the foundation for exceptional flavor and texture. It is impossible to emphasize the importance of selecting premium ingredients while making holiday cookies. The first cardinal rule in this culinary expedition is to prioritize fresh and seasonal produce. Fruits like cranberries and citrus, nuts, and spices are at their prime during the winter months, imparting a vibrancy and robustness to your cookies that is simply unparalleled.

Equally vital is the quality of the flour, the backbone of any baking endeavor. Opting for a high-quality, unbleached all-purpose flour ensures a clean, pure taste without the chemical residue that can accompany bleached alternatives. Additionally, incorporating alternative flours such as almond or oat flour can elevate the nutritional profile of your cookies while adding distinct flavors and textures. When it comes to sweeteners, choosing premium options like organic brown sugar or molasses enhances the depth of your cookie's flavor. It aligns with the ethos of creating an indulgent and consciously crafted treat.

The dairy aisle is another realm where the quality of ingredients can make a substantial difference. Opting for farm-fresh eggs contributes to the ethical treatment of animals and enhances the richness and color of your cookies. Selecting unsalted, high-quality butter is paramount; its rich, creamy texture and pure flavor are central to achieving that melt-in-your-mouth goodness that defines exceptional holiday treats. The incorporation of dairy, be it in the form of milk, cream, or yogurt, should also prioritize freshness and quality to ensure a superior final product.

In the realm of flavor extracts, the choice of vanilla extract can significantly impact the overall taste of your cookies. Opting for pure vanilla extract derived from vanilla beans imparts a depth of flavor beyond the sweetness of artificial quotes. Vanilla becomes the symphony conductor, orchestrating the harmonious blending of various ingredients to create a cohesive and delightful composition. For those seeking to infuse a touch of holiday spirit, experimenting with high-quality almond or peppermint extracts can add a layer of complexity and festivity to your cookie repertoire.

Spices, those aromatic flavor ambassadors, deserve special attention in the ingredient selection process. The quality and freshness of cinnamon, nutmeg, cloves, and other seasonal spices can elevate your cookies from ordinary to extraordinary. Investing in whole spices and grinding them just before use ensures an intensity of flavor that pre-ground counterparts often need to improve. This attention to detail transforms your cookies into aromatic masterpieces, each bite redolent with the essence of winter.

Nuts, a beloved addition to many holiday cookie recipes, should be carefully chosen. Opting for fresh, high-quality nuts and toasting them before use enhances their flavor and adds a delightful crunch to your cookies. Whether it's the buttery richness of almonds, the earthy notes of walnuts, or the sweet crunch of pecans, the right choice and preparation of nuts can elevate your cookies to a level of indulgence that resonates with the season's spirit.

When aiming for the ultimate taste, it is imperative to utilize fresh citrus zest sparingly. Selecting juicy, fragrant citrus fruits and meticulously grating the peels adds a sharp contrast to the richness of the cookie dough. The oils in citrus zest contribute to flavor and the overall olfactory experience, creating cookies that are as delightful to smell as they are to taste.

The choice extends beyond brown sugar and molasses in the realm of sweeteners. Experimenting with alternative sweeteners like honey or maple syrup can introduce nuanced flavors that complement the other ingredients. It's essential, however, to consider the viscosity and sweetness levels of these alternatives and adjust your recipe accordingly. The quest for quality extends beyond taste to the ethical and environmental aspects of the ingredients. Opting for organic and sustainably sourced ingredients whenever possible aligns with a conscious approach to baking, ensuring that your culinary creations not only delight the palate but also reflect a commitment to responsible consumption.

Freshness and quality also extend to the realm of dried fruits. Choosing plump, moist specimens enhances your cookies' texture and flavor, whether it's cranberries, apricots, figs, or dates. Dried fruits should be treated as a star ingredient rather than an afterthought, contributing their unique sweetness and chewiness to the overall composition.

While it may be tempting to rely solely on convenience, the extra effort to select high-quality ingredients pays dividends in the final result. Avoiding processed and overly refined ingredients allows the inherent flavors of each component to shine, resulting in cookies that are not only delicious but also a testament to the craftsmanship of the baker. To pursue excellence, consider exploring specialty stores and farmers' markets where you may find unique, artisanal ingredients that can add a distinctive touch to your holiday creations.

In conclusion, selecting quality ingredients is the cornerstone of successful holiday cookie baking. Each component plays a crucial role in the symphony of flavors that defines exceptional cookies, from the spices that weave a tapestry of warmth to the butter that imparts richness. As you embark on your baking journey, let the commitment to quality be your guiding principle, and may each carefully chosen ingredient contribute to creating holiday treats that delight the senses and embody the season's magic.

Emphasizing the flavors of winter

With its crisp air and frost-kissed landscapes, winter beckons a symphony of flavors that evoke warmth, comfort, and festive spirit. As we embark on the culinary adventure of holiday baking, the art lies not only in the ingredients themselves but in the skillful orchestration of flavors that capture the season's essence. At the heart of this endeavor is a dance with spices, where cinnamon, nutmeg, and cloves take center stage. These warming spices, reminiscent of crackling fires and snug evenings by the hearth, infuse winter treats with a nostalgic aroma that immediately transports us to the heart of the holidays. The judicious use of these spices, often called the trinity of winter baking, elevates cookies from mere confections to sensory experiences, where each bite carries the comforting essence of a winter's day.

In the embrace of winter, citrus fruits emerge as bright, zesty ambassadors of freshness. Oranges, lemons, and limes lend a burst of sunshine to holiday treats, cutting through the richness of cookie doughs with their lively acidity. The zest of citrus fruits, rich in essential oils, becomes a secret weapon, infusing cookies with a fragrant and uplifting quality that mirrors the crispness of winter air. The combination of citrus and winter spices creates a nuanced harmony, balancing the warmth of cinnamon with the bright, refreshing notes of citrus, resulting in both comforting and refreshing cookies.

Nuts, with their earthy richness, add a layer of complexity to winter treats. Almonds, walnuts, and pecans, whether finely ground or coarsely chopped, bring a satisfying crunch that mirrors the crispness of winter mornings. Toasting these nuts before incorporating them into recipes intensifies their flavor, imparting a warm and toasty undertone that resonates with the comforting ambiance of the season. The marriage of nuts and winter spices, as seen in classics like cinnamon-spiced almond cookies or nut-studded gingerbread, creates a synergy that defines winter treats' robust and indulgent character.

The season's bountiful harvest of fresh and dried fruits also plays a pivotal role in emphasizing winter flavors. With their ruby-red hue and tartness, Cranberries become a quintessential winter ingredient, infusing cookies with a burst of color and a lively tang. When paired with orange zest or spices, cranberries contribute to a dynamic flavor profile that mirrors the contrast of winter landscapes. Dried fruits such as apricots, figs, and dates, with their concentrated sweetness and chewy texture, offer a decadent counterpoint, enhancing winter treats' overall depth and richness.

The dairy aisle, too, embraces the season's spirit, with butter taking on a special significance. Premium unsalted butter is a blank canvas for the winter flavors to apply. Its rich, creamy taste imparts a luxurious quality to cookies, creating a melt-in-your-mouth texture that defines classic holiday treats. The choice of butter extends beyond mere functionality; it becomes a deliberate decision to elevate the flavor profile of each cookie, ensuring that the essence of winter is not only tasted but savored.

In the realm of extracts, vanilla, that timeless and versatile flavor, finds its place in the winter symphony. Pure vanilla extract, derived from the beans of the vanilla orchid, adds a sweet and floral note that complements the complexity of winter spices. The warmth of vanilla becomes the bridge that ties together various elements, creating a cohesive and harmonious flavor profile in cookies. For those seeking to infuse a touch of holiday spirit, almond, and peppermint extracts make enchanting appearances, adding layers of depth and festivity to the winter repertoire.

As the holiday season unfolds, alternative flours like almond or oat flour make a compelling entrance, offering gluten-free options and introducing unique textures and flavors to winter treats. With their nutty undertones and wholesome qualities, these flours contribute to the overall complexity of cookies, ensuring every bite is a journey through diverse and delightful flavors.

The emphasis on winter flavors extends to the realm of sweeteners, where the choice of brown sugar and molasses becomes a deliberate nod to the comforting and robust qualities of the season. Brown sugar, with its molasses content, adds depth and moisture to cookie dough, contributing to a chewy and tender texture. With its rich, complex sweetness and hint of caramel, Molasses becomes a key player in gingerbread and molasses cookies, infusing them with a distinctive winter character.

Winter's charms don't stop in the kitchen; they also permeate the beverage industry, changing cookie flavor profiles. Tea-infused cookies are refined and fragrant, with the subtle aromas of chai or Earl Grey skillfully combined with winter spices. Similarly, incorporating seasonal ingredients like hot cocoa mix or mulled wine spices introduces a playful and festive dimension to winter treats, transforming them into edible reflections of beloved winter traditions.

The skill of highlighting winter flavors in cookies is a subtle ballet of proportions and combinations, not limited to single components. It's about finding the sweet spot where the warmth of spices harmonizes with the brightness of citrus, where the richness of nuts complements the tartness of cranberries, and where the indulgence of butter meets the complexity of molasses. In this culinary waltz, the baker becomes a maestro, conducting a symphony of tastes that resonate with the soul-warming sensations of winter.

Beyond the sensory pleasure, emphasizing winter flavors in cookies becomes a way to connect with tradition and evoke a sense of nostalgia. The aromas that waft through the kitchen and the flavors that linger on the palate all become vessels of memory, transporting us to snowy days, festive gatherings, and the timeless joy of the holiday season. As we savor each bite of a winter-spiced cookie, we celebrate flavors that transcend the act of eating; it becomes a communion with the season itself.

In conclusion, the emphasis on winter flavors in holiday cookies is a celebration of the richness and diversity that the season brings. It's a deliberate and thoughtful curation of ingredients, a symphony of spices, fruits, nuts, and extracts that transform each cookie into a masterpiece of winter indulgence. As you embark on your winter baking adventures, let the season's flavors guide your creativity, and may each cookie be a testament to the magic, warmth, and joy that winter brings.

CHAPTER II

Essential Baking Tools and Techniques

Overview of necessary tools

Embarking on the enchanting journey of holiday cookie baking requires a passion for the art and a well-equipped kitchen with the necessary tools. These tools serve as unsung heroes, facilitating precision, efficiency, and the seamless execution of delightful recipes. At the heart of the cookie-making endeavor lies the humble mixer, whether a stand or a hand mixer. This indispensable tool transforms the laborious task of creaming butter and sugar into a breeze, ensuring a uniform and velvety consistency that is the foundation of many classic cookies. The rhythmic hum of the mixer becomes a symphony conductor, orchestrating the harmony of ingredients to perfection.

Accuracy is paramount in measuring, and a set of reliable measuring cups and spoons become the baker's trusted companions. Precise measurements guarantee the recipe's success and contribute to the science of baking, where the correct ratios of ingredients are crucial to achieving the desired texture and flavor. A digital kitchen scale further elevates precision, especially when dealing with ingredients like flour, where slight variations in quantity can significantly impact the final product.

As the cookie dough takes shape, the rolling pin emerges as a wielded wand, transforming the dough into a canvas ready for creative expression. Whether crafting delicate cut-out cookies or shaping uniform balls for drop cookies, the rolling pin becomes an extension of the baker's hands, providing the control and finesse necessary for achieving the desired thickness and texture.

Cookie cutters cut through the dough, serving as sculptor's tools for defining holiday delicacies with their festive shapes. From traditional gingerbread men to intricate snowflakes and Christmas trees, the variety of cookie cutters allows for endless possibilities, turning cookie-making into a delightful form of edible artistry. Silpat baking mats or parchment paper, laid on baking sheets, ensure that cookies release effortlessly and that cleanup is a breeze while preventing excessive browning on the bottom.

The oven, a magician's chamber in the alchemy of baking, must be calibrated to perfection. An oven thermometer becomes essential, offering an accurate reading that ensures cookies bake at the intended temperature. This seemingly simple device provides consistent results, preventing the disappointment of undercooked or over-baked cookies. Baking sheets, preferably heavy-duty and of good quality, distribute heat evenly. At the same time, cooling racks allow for proper cooling, preventing the dreaded sogginess that can occur when cookies cool on the baking sheet.

In cookie decoration, piping bags and tips become the artist's brush, allowing for intricate designs and creative expressions. Royal icing, the painter's palette, takes on the role of both adhesive and embellishment, transforming plain cookies into canvases for festive designs. Cookie decorators often employ a variety of tips to achieve different effects, from delicate lines to intricate rosettes, adding a layer of visual delight to holiday treats.

Cookie stamps or embossing tools offer an alternative avenue for creativity, imprinting designs onto the cookie's surface before baking. This is an excellent substitute for those looking for a more straightforward yet still elegant manner because it adds a decorative element without requiring a sophisticated icing process. Decorating pens and edible glitter further enhance the artistic possibilities, allowing for the addition of fine details and a touch of sparkle that elevates cookies to a level of sophistication.

Beyond the tools designed explicitly for cookie making, the well-equipped kitchen also encompasses a range of general tools that enhance efficiency and ease during baking. Silicone spatulas prove invaluable for scraping every last bit of cookie dough from mixing bowls, ensuring minimal waste and optimal use of ingredients. A reliable set of whisks aids in preparing various batters, from the light and fluffy to the thick and rich. Pastry brushes become versatile instruments for applying egg washes, spreading melted butter, or dusting cookies with powdered sugar.

Cookie scoops, available in various sizes, revolutionize the shaping process, ensuring uniformity in size and helping to maintain consistent baking times. These scoops streamline the production of drop cookies and contribute to the aesthetic appeal of evenly sized and perfectly round cookies. The cookie scoop becomes a time-saving ally, especially when faced with large batches of dough during the holiday baking frenzy.

In the modern era, technology joins the kitchen brigade with the advent of digital timers and smart thermometers. Timer devices make sure cookies are taken out of the oven precisely, guard against inadvertently leaving them in there, and emit a variety of alarms. Digital thermometers, with instant and accurate readings, eliminate the guesswork associated with testing cookie doneness, providing confidence and precision in the baking process.

Storage containers, an often-overlooked tool, have become essential in preserving the freshness and flavor of baked cookies. Airtight containers or cookie tins shield cookies from moisture and air, preventing them from becoming stale. These containers also play a crucial role in storing decorated cookies, protecting delicate icing work from smudging or sticking.

The overview of necessary tools for holiday cookie baking unveils a carefully curated ensemble designed to transform the kitchen into a haven of creativity and precision. Armed with these tools, the baker becomes a maestro, conducting a symphony of ingredients and techniques to produce cookies that delight the taste buds and enchant the eyes. As each tool takes its place in this culinary orchestra, the magic of holiday baking comes to life, turning the kitchen into a realm where simple ingredients are transformed into edible masterpieces, ready to usher in the festive spirit.

Basic baking techniques

Mastering the art of holiday cookie baking involves selecting the finest ingredients and honing fundamental baking techniques that form the backbone of every successful recipe. At the forefront of these techniques is the crucial skill of accurate measuring. The precision of ingredients, from flour and sugar to spices and extracts, plays a pivotal role in achieving cookies' desired texture and flavor. Measuring cups and spoons become the trusted allies in this pursuit, ensuring that each component is carefully proportioned and contributes harmoniously to the final product.

Creaming is a fundamental technique that sets the stage for many cookie recipes. The process of beating butter and sugar together, whether using a stand mixer, a hand mixer, or even the old-fashioned wooden spoon, is transformative. It introduces air into the mixture, creating a light and fluffy base that serves as the foundation for many classic cookies. The creaming technique contributes to the texture and facilitates the even distribution of flavors, ensuring a consistent taste throughout each cookie.

Once the dough comes together, rolling and shaping take center stage. A well-floured surface and a reliable rolling pin become essential tools in crafting the perfect thickness for cut-out cookies. The evenness of the dough ensures uniform baking, preventing some cookies from becoming too crisp while others remain underbaked. With their varied shapes and sizes, cookie cutters lend a festive touch, allowing bakers to unleash their creativity and personalize their treats for different occasions.

The judicious use of leavening agents, such as baking powder and baking soda, contributes to the rise and texture of cookies. Understanding the role of these agents and their interaction with acidic or alkaline ingredients is crucial in achieving the desired lift. Overusing leavening agents can lead to overly puffy or cake-like cookies, while insufficient amounts may result in dense and flat treats. Striking the right balance ensures cookies have the perfect crumb and texture.

Temperature management is a fundamental aspect of successful baking. Preheating the oven allows cookies to start baking immediately, ensuring that they set correctly and achieve the desired structure. Consistent oven temperatures are equally important; an oven thermometer becomes the baker's ally in verifying that the temperature matches the recipe instructions. Proper temperature control prevents uneven baking, ensuring each cookie in a batch emerges with a uniform golden hue.

The timing of baking is an art in itself. Knowing when to remove cookies from the oven requires attention to visual cues and sensory indicators. When the edges are just beginning to turn golden, the cookies have cooked all the way through without being overdone. Because they will continue to set as they cool on the baking sheet, the cookies should feel firm around the edges but still soft in the middle. A digital timer is essential for preventing underbaked or overbaked biscuits because timing is a delicate dance.

Cooling is the unsung hero in the final stages of baking. Allowing cookies to cool on the baking sheet for a few minutes before transferring them to a wire rack prevents them from becoming misshapen or sticking. The gradual cooling process contributes to developing the desired texture, preventing cookies from becoming too crisp or soft. This stage rewards patience with aesthetically pleasing cookies with the perfect chewiness and crispness.

The art of decorating cookies introduces various techniques that elevate them from simple treats to edible works of art. Royal icing becomes a versatile medium for creating intricate designs with its smooth and glossy finish. The flooding technique involves outlining the cookie with a thicker icing before flooding the interior with a thinner consistency, resulting in a seamless and polished look. Piping and flooding techniques allow for the creation of intricate patterns while adding edible glitter, sanding sugar, or dragees, which add a touch of sparkle and texture.

For those who prefer a more straightforward yet equally charming approach, cookie stamps or embossing tools offer an easy way to imprint festive designs onto the cookie's surface before baking. This technique adds visual interest without the need for intricate icing work, making it an accessible option for novice and experienced bakers alike. Using colored sugars, sprinkles, and nonpareils provides additional avenues for creativity, allowing bakers to customize their cookies to suit the theme or occasion.

Understanding the principles of flavor infusion is a subtler yet equally essential technique. Incorporating fresh citrus zest or spices into the dough introduces nuanced flavors that permeate each bite. Toasting nuts before adding them to the dough enhances their richness, contributing a warm and toasty undertone. Experimenting with alternative flours, such as almond or oat flour, not only accommodates dietary preferences but also introduces unique textures and flavors. Mastering the art of flavor infusion allows bakers to tailor their cookies to suit individual tastes, creating a diverse array of treats catering to various palates.

Storage techniques ensure that the freshness and flavor of cookies endure beyond the initial baking. Airtight containers or cookie tins shield cookies from moisture and air, preventing them from becoming stale. For decorated cookies, layers of parchment or wax paper between each layer prevent the designs from smudging or sticking. Proper storage is practical for preserving the quality of cookies and allows for preparing batches in advance, reducing the stress of last-minute baking during the holiday season.

Understanding common issues and their solutions becomes an invaluable skill in cookie troubleshooting. Overmixing, for example, can lead to tough cookies due to excessive gluten development. The remedy lies in gentle mixing and incorporating dry ingredients until combined. Spreading issues, where cookies lose their intended shape during baking, may result from overly soft dough—chilling the dough before baking resolves this problem, allowing cookies to hold their form. Familiarity with common pitfalls equips bakers with the knowledge to troubleshoot and refine their techniques, ensuring consistent success in every batch.

In conclusion, mastering basic baking techniques lays the foundation for creating exquisite holiday cookies. From accurate measuring and precise creaming to the art of rolling, shaping, and decorating, each method contributes to the alchemy of turning simple ingredients into delightful treats. Temperature control, timing, and cooling are the subtle yet critical stages that ensure cookies emerge from the oven with the perfect texture and flavor. As bakers navigate the world of holiday cookie baking, these techniques become the tools of their craft, allowing for creating not just cookies but edible masterpieces that capture the spirit of the season.

Tips for success in holiday cookie baking

Holiday cookie baking is an art that combines tradition, creativity, and a touch of magic. Achieving success in this delightful endeavor requires a passion for the craft and a set of tried-and-true tips that can elevate your cookies from good to exceptional. The journey begins with careful planning and organization. Before diving into the world of flour and sugar, take the time to review recipes, assemble ingredients, and ensure that all necessary tools are within reach. This initial stage expedites the baking procedure and lessens the aggravation of discovering mid-recipe that an essential element needs to be added.

Understanding your recipes is fundamental to success. Familiarize yourself with the steps, ingredients, and any specific techniques required. If you're trying a new recipe, read through it thoroughly before starting to ensure that you grasp the nuances. This awareness not only enhances confidence but also allows for creativity within the framework of the recipe. Additionally, take note of any variations in ingredient temperatures. For example, when recipes call for softened butter or room-temperature eggs, allowing these ingredients to come to the specified temperature ensures proper emulsification and a uniform texture in your dough.

Precision in measuring is a cornerstone of successful baking. Invest in quality measuring cups and spoons, and level off dry ingredients to ensure accurate quantities. This precision extends to the measuring of flour, where the scoop-and-level method prevents overpacking and results in a consistent texture. A digital kitchen scale can be an invaluable tool, especially when measuring ingredients like flour, where slight variations in quantity can significantly impact the final product.

In the realm of ingredient selection, prioritize quality. Opt for fresh and seasonal produce, and choose high-quality butter, spices, and extracts. The flavor of your cookies is only as good as the ingredients you use, so don't be afraid to invest in premium options. Experimenting with alternative flours, like almond or oat flour, can introduce unique textures and flavors while catering to dietary preferences. Remember to consider the influence of small details, such as the choice of vanilla extract or the freshness of nuts, in shaping the overall taste profile of your cookies.

Temperature control is a critical factor in successful cookie baking. Before putting cookies inside, ensure your oven is preheated to the appropriate temperature. An oven thermometer can be a valuable tool for verifying accuracy, as oven temperatures vary. Understanding your oven's nuances and making slight adjustments can make a significant difference for cookies that require a specific level of crispiness or chewiness. Additionally, chilling cookie dough before baking can prevent excessive spreading, ensuring that your cookies maintain their intended shape.

Cookie scoops in various sizes offer a practical and efficient way to portion dough, resulting in uniformly sized cookies. This contributes to a visually appealing presentation and ensures consistent baking times. Experiment with different scoop sizes to achieve your cookies' desired size and thickness. Silicone baking mats or parchment paper on baking sheets prevent cookies from sticking and aid in even baking and easy cleanup. These small details contribute to a seamless baking experience.

Experimenting with different mixing techniques allows for customizing your cookies' texture. The creaming method, where butter and sugar are beaten until light and fluffy, creates a tender and cakey texture. The reverse creaming process adds dry ingredients to the fat, resulting in a denser and chewier texture. Understanding these techniques empowers you to tailor your cookies to suit personal preferences and desired outcomes.

Timing is an art in cookie baking. Invest in a reliable digital timer and closely monitor your cookies during the final minutes of baking. Cookies continue to set as they cool on the baking sheet, so resist the temptation to leave them in the oven for too long. Achieving the perfect balance between a golden edge and a slightly soft center requires finesse and attentiveness. Trust your senses— visual cues, a gentle touch, and the aroma of baking cookies—to guide you to the ideal moment for removing them from the oven.

Cooling is an often underestimated step in the baking process. Allowing cookies to cool on the baking sheet for a few minutes before transferring them to a wire rack prevents them from becoming misshapen or sticking. This gradual cooling process contributes to developing the desired texture, preventing cookies from becoming too crisp or soft. Be patient during this stage, as it ensures that your cookies are visually appealing and boast an ideal balance of crispiness and chewiness.

The world of cookie decoration opens up a realm of creative possibilities. Royal icing becomes a versatile medium for creating intricate designs with its smooth and glossy finish. If you're new to cookie decorating, start with simple techniques like flooding and piping before venturing into more complicated procedures. Use edible markers, food coloring, and edible glitter to add personalized touches to your cookies. For those who prefer a more straightforward yet equally charming approach, cookie stamps or embossing tools offer an easy way to imprint festive designs onto the cookie's surface before baking. This technique adds visual interest without the need for intricate icing work, making it an accessible option for novice and experienced bakers alike.

Storage techniques ensure that the freshness and flavor of cookies endure beyond the initial baking. Airtight containers or cookie tins shield cookies from moisture and air, preventing them from becoming stale. For decorated cookies, layers of parchment or wax paper between each layer prevent the designs from smudging or sticking. Proper storage is practical for preserving the quality of cookies and allows for preparing batches in advance, reducing the stress of last-minute baking during the holiday season.

Understanding common issues and their solutions becomes an invaluable skill in cookie troubleshooting. Overmixing, for example, can lead to tough cookies due to excessive gluten development. The remedy lies in gentle mixing and incorporating dry ingredients until combined. Spreading issues, where cookies lose their intended shape during baking, may result from overly soft dough—chilling the dough before baking resolves this problem, allowing cookies to hold their form. Familiarity with common pitfalls equips bakers with the knowledge to troubleshoot and refine their techniques, ensuring consistent success in every batch.

Finally, embrace the spirit of creativity and enjoyment. Holiday cookie baking is not just about precision and technique; it's a joyful expression of love and tradition. Feel free to experiment with flavors, decorations, and new recipes. Share the experience with loved ones, involve family and friends in baking, and make it a memorable and festive occasion. The beauty of holiday cookie baking lies not only in the delicious treats that emerge from the oven but also in the joy, warmth, and traditions it fosters in your home.

CHAPTER III

Classic Holiday Cookie Recipes

Sugar cookies with festive decorations

Sugar cookies adorned with festive decorations symbolize holiday joy and culinary tradition. With their tender crumb and subtly sweet flavor, these delightful treats are a blank canvas for creative expression during the festive season. The journey begins with a simple yet foundational sugar cookie recipe that forms the basis for many shapes, sizes, and decorative possibilities. The key is to get the ideal ratio of ingredients: flour for structure, sugar for sweetness, butter for richness, and a dash of vanilla for flavor depth. This well-balanced recipe yields a flexible dough that can be molded, rolled, and cut into various festive forms.

The rolling out of sugar cookie dough becomes a ritual that captures the essence of holiday baking. A floured surface and a trusty rolling pin transform the dough into a malleable sheet, ready to be adorned with festive shapes. Cookie cutters add a touch of whimsy, ranging from classic holiday symbols like snowflakes, Christmas trees, and gingerbread men to personalized figures that reflect individual creativity. Cutting out each cookie becomes a celebration of tradition and anticipation, setting the stage for the following artistic endeavors.

Once baked to a delicate golden hue, the sugar cookies become a blank canvas awaiting festive transformations. Royal icing becomes the artist's medium of choice with its smooth texture and glossy finish. Flooded onto each cookie with precision, royal icing creates a seamless canvas for intricate designs and vibrant colors. The flooding technique gives cookies a sleek and finished look. It involves pipetting the cookie's outline with a thicker icing and flooding the center with a thinner consistency. This method not only provides a flawless surface for decorating but also serves as the adhesive for additional embellishments.

Piping and flooding techniques open up a world of creative possibilities. Delicate lines, intricate patterns, and vibrant colors come to life as bakers wield piping bags with finesse. Cookie decorators often employ various tips, each contributing to a different effect, from fine detailing to broader strokes. Adding edible markers, food coloring, and edible glitter enhances the visual appeal, allowing for the personalization of each cookie. In this artistic process, sugar cookies with festive decorations transcend their role as mere treats and become edible works of art that embody the holiday spirit.

For those who prefer a more straightforward yet equally charming approach, cookie stamps or embossing tools offer an accessible yet visually appealing option. These tools imprint festive designs onto the cookie's surface before baking, adding a decorative touch without requiring intricate icing work. This technique not only saves time but also appeals to those who appreciate the beauty of simplicity. Colored sugars, sprinkles, and nonpareils provide additional avenues for creativity, allowing bakers to customize their cookies to suit the theme or occasion.

Decorating sugar cookies becomes a communal and joyous affair, making it a popular activity during holiday gatherings. Families, friends, and even co-workers come together to partake in the creative process, transforming plain cookies into vibrant and personalized expressions of holiday cheer. The decorating table becomes a happy place where memories are created, and traditions are passed down through the years when it is covered in sprinkles, icing colors, and other decorative embellishments.

Beyond their visual appeal, sugar cookies with festive decorations engage the senses in a holistic experience. The aroma of freshly baked cookies, tinged with the sweetness of vanilla and the warm notes of butter, fills the kitchen and lingers in the air. Biting into a sugar cookie reveals a delicate crunch, followed by the tender crumb that melts in the mouth. The combination of textures— the crispness of the icing, the slight resistance of the cookie, and the crunch of embellishments—creates a sensory symphony that transcends taste alone.

The tradition of gifting decorated sugar cookies adds a layer of sentiment to these festive treats. Beautifully packaged and adorned with ribbons or festive wrappings, these cookies become tokens of affection and thoughtfulness. Whether shared with neighbors, exchanged among friends, or presented as hostess gifts, decorated sugar cookies carry with them the spirit of the season and the joy of giving. Gifting becomes a way to share cookies and the love and warmth associated with the holidays.

As sugar cookies with festive decorations grace holiday gatherings and cookie exchanges, they become not just treats but storytellers. Each cookie carries the narrative of the baker's creativity, the joy of shared moments, and the beauty of traditions passed down through generations. The legacy of sugar cookies with festive decorations extends beyond their brief existence; it lives on in the memories created, the laughter shared, and the enduring traditions woven into the fabric of the holiday season.

In the modern era, the art of decorating sugar cookies has found a new platform through social media. Platforms like Instagram and Pinterest showcase various stunning creations, inspiring bakers worldwide to push the boundaries of creativity. Cookie decorators have become influencers, sharing their recipes, techniques, and stories behind each design. This digital age has transformed sugar cookies into edible art, transcending geographical boundaries and connecting a global community of bakers and enthusiasts.

While decorating sugar cookies is often associated with joy and creativity, it can also present challenges that require patience and practice. Achieving the right consistency of royal icing, mastering piping techniques, and ensuring that each cookie receives an even layer of icing are skills that develop over time. The potential for cookies to spread unevenly or for icing to run poses additional challenges. However, it's in navigating these challenges that decorators discover the resilience and adaptability required in culinary artistry.

In conclusion, sugar cookies with festive decorations epitomize the magic and tradition of holiday baking. The process celebrates creativity, love, and shared moments, from the careful rolling out of dough to the artistic embellishments that adorn each cookie. These cookies, whether enjoyed as a personal indulgence, shared in festive gatherings, or gifted with thoughtfulness, carry the season's essence. Beyond their visual appeal and delicious taste, sugar cookies with festive decorations embody the joy of holiday traditions, the warmth of shared experiences, and the timeless beauty of edible art.

Gingerbread cookies with royal icing

Gingerbread cookies adorned with intricate designs of royal icing embody the quintessential spirit of the holiday season. Gingerbread cookies, rooted in centuries-old customs, have come to represent coziness, fond memories, and joyous occasions. The trip starts with a traditional recipe for gingerbread cookies, a tasteful combination of ginger, molasses, brown sugar, and spices. The rich, spicy scent of the holidays fills the kitchen with this aromatic blend that captures the spirit of the occasion.

Making gingerbread cookies is more than a culinary venture; it's a sensory experience that engages sight, smell, and touch. The dough, infused with the warmth of ginger, cinnamon, and cloves, becomes a tactile canvas for creative expression. Rolling out the dough on a floured surface and cutting it into various shapes with gingerbread men, trees, and stars as popular choices initiates the transformation from raw ingredients to delightful forms ready for baking.

Once the golden brown and fragrant gingerbread shapes emerge from the oven, they are a blank canvas awaiting the artistic touch of royal icing. Royal icing, a simple yet versatile mixture of confectioners' sugar, egg whites, and a touch of lemon juice, becomes the magical substance that transforms each cookie into a work of edible art. Its smooth texture, glossy finish, and quick-drying properties make it the ideal medium for creating intricate designs and festive patterns.

The foundation for decorating gingerbread cookies is the technique known as flooding, which involves covering the cookie's surface with a thin layer of royal icing. This technique provides a smooth canvas for additional details and is the adhesive for embellishments. Piping, a delicate and precise process, allows decorators to add intricate lines, patterns, and designs. The fine tip of a piping bag becomes a brush in the hands of a gingerbread artist, weaving stories of holiday cheer and whimsy on each cookie.

Gingerbread cookies' timeless appeal invites diverse designs that reflect tradition and creativity. Classic motifs like snowflakes, holly leaves, and candy canes evoke a sense of nostalgia, harkening back to a bygone era of holiday charm. Intricate lace-like patterns inspired by Scandinavian traditions add a touch of elegance and sophistication to gingerbread creations. Personalized designs, from family initials to festive scenes, showcase the versatility of gingerbread as a medium for edible storytelling.

Decorating gingerbread cookies becomes a communal and festive affair, often shared among family and friends. Gingerbread decorating parties, where individuals gather to adorn cookies with unique designs, have become a cherished tradition. The decorating table, filled with royal icing colors, sprinkles, edible pearls, and other embellishments, becomes a miniature workshop where holiday magic happens. In these moments of shared creativity, gingerbread cookies transcend their role as mere sweets and become edible tokens of joy and togetherness.

Beyond their aesthetic allure, gingerbread cookies engage the taste buds in a dance of flavors that epitomize the essence of the holiday season. The spiciness of ginger, the warmth of cinnamon, and the depth of molasses create a symphony of tastes that evoke memories of festive gatherings, cozy evenings by the fire, and the joy of indulging in holiday treats. The subtle sweetness of royal icing, with its delicate hint of lemon, complements the robust flavors of gingerbread, striking a harmonious balance that enhances the overall experience.

Gingerbread cookies with royal icing extend their impact beyond individual indulgence to become tokens of affection and goodwill. Beautifully packaged and adorned with festive wrappings, these cookies transform into thoughtful gifts that carry the season's spirit. Whether exchanged among friends, presented as hostess gifts, or shared with neighbors, gingerbread cookies become tangible expressions of love and festive cheer. Gifting gingerbread cookies becomes a gesture of warmth and hospitality, fostering a sense of community and connection during the holiday season.

The tradition of gingerbread cookies with royal icing extends back centuries, with roots in medieval Europe. Gingerbread, initially a specialty of skilled bakers, evolved into a popular treat associated with festivities, celebrations, and even religious occasions. The cookies were often shaped into elaborate forms, including figures of kings, queens, and animals, and decorated with colored icing. Over time, gingerbread became synonymous with the holiday season, with gingerbread houses and decorated cookies adorning festive tables and capturing the imaginations of generations.

In recent years, gingerbread cookie decorating has experienced a renaissance, partly thanks to the rise of social media platforms. Instagram, Pinterest, and other platforms showcase a dazzling array of gingerbread creations, from intricately detailed scenes to whimsical characters. Gingerbread artists, both amateur and professional, share their designs, techniques, and stories, inspiring a global community of bakers to push the boundaries of creativity. The digital age has transformed gingerbread cookies into edible art, fostering a sense of camaraderie among enthusiasts worldwide.

While decorating gingerbread cookies is often associated with joy and creativity, it also presents challenges that require patience and practice. Achieving the right consistency of royal icing, mastering piping techniques, and ensuring that each cookie receives an even layer of icing are skills that develop over time. The potential for cookies to spread unevenly or for icing to run poses additional challenges. However, it's in navigating these challenges that decorators discover the resilience and adaptability required in culinary artistry.

In conclusion, gingerbread cookies with royal icing are enduring symbols of holiday joy, tradition, and creativity. Each step celebrates the season, from the aromatic journey of creating the gingerbread dough to the meticulous artistry of royal icing designs. These cookies, whether displayed as festive decorations, shared in gatherings, or gifted with love, carry the magic of the holidays. Gingerbread cookies with royal icing engage the senses in a symphony of flavors and aromas and serve as edible canvases for the artistic expression of holiday cheer, capturing the essence of festive traditions and the timeless joy of sharing edible works of art.

Peppermint chocolate chip cookies

Peppermint chocolate chip cookies stand as delectable holiday ambassadors with their enchanting fusion of cool mint and rich chocolate. These cookies, a marriage of classic chocolate chip goodness with the refreshing essence of peppermint, offer a sensory journey that captures the spirit of festive celebrations. The journey begins with a foundational chocolate chip cookie recipe, where the buttery sweetness of traditional dough sets the stage for the introduction of peppermint. As the familiar ingredients—flour, sugar, butter, and eggs—come together, adding peppermint extract and finely crushed candy canes elevates the dough to a realm of seasonal delight.

The scent of peppermint chocolate chip cookies baking in the oven is a sensory symphony that signals the arrival of holiday joy. The mingling aromas of melting chocolate and cool mint fill the kitchen, creating an olfactory experience that transports enthusiasts to memories of cozy evenings, festive gatherings, and the warmth of holiday traditions. The anticipation builds as the cookies transform from mounds of dough to golden delights, with each chocolate chip glistening and each subtle hint of crushed peppermint promising a burst of flavor.

The cooling process is a crucial phase in creating peppermint chocolate chip cookies. As they settle on the baking sheet, the cookies transform, developing a chewy yet tender texture that marries the classic attributes of chocolate chip cookies with the refreshing coolness of peppermint. The peppermint chips, dispersed throughout the dough, provide delightful pockets of refreshing flavor that complement the rich decadence of the chocolate chips. The harmonious interplay of these contrasting elements defines the uniqueness of peppermint chocolate chip cookies.

Biting into a peppermint chocolate chip cookie is a journey of textures and tastes. The initial crunch of the outer layer gives way to a soft and chewy interior, where the melted chocolate and peppermint chips meld together in a dance of flavors. The coolness of peppermint offers a refreshing contrast to the cookie's sweetness, creating a harmonious balance that lingers on the palate. It's a symphony of textures and tastes that resonates with the festive spirit, making each bite a moment of pure indulgence.

Peppermint chocolate chip cookies extend beyond their deliciousness to become a visual delight. The vibrant contrast of red and white peppermint chips against the rich backdrop of chocolate chips creates a festive mosaic that mirrors the season's colors. The cookies, with their golden-brown edges and studded with colorful chips, become edible ornaments that add a touch of holiday cheer to any gathering. The visual appeal of peppermint chocolate chip cookies makes them a treat for the taste buds and a feast for the eyes, enhancing the overall experience of indulging in these festive delights.

The versatility of peppermint chocolate chip cookies extends to their presentation and serving. Whether displayed in a cookie jar, arranged on a festive platter, or packaged as delightful gifts, these cookies become edible works of art that contribute to the visual ambiance of holiday celebrations. The simple act of sharing peppermint chocolate chip cookies becomes a gesture of spreading joy and warmth. Presented in decorative tins or adorned with festive ribbons, these cookies become tokens of affection that encapsulate the spirit of giving during the holiday season.

Beyond their role as standalone treats, peppermint chocolate chip cookies become versatile ingredients in holiday desserts and creations. Crumbled into ice cream, folded into brownie batter, or sandwiched between layers of peppermint-infused frosting, these cookies lend their distinctive flavors to various confections. The creative possibilities expand as bakers experiment with incorporating peppermint chocolate chip cookies into truffles, milkshakes, or even a peppermint bark parfait. The adaptability of these cookies invites culinary exploration, allowing enthusiasts to infuse their favorite holiday recipes with the refreshing essence of peppermint and the richness of chocolate.

The custom of peppermint chocolate chip cookies aligns with the joyful traditions that have become integral to the holiday season. Baking sessions, where families and friends gather in the kitchen to create batches of these cookies, have become a cherished part of seasonal rituals. Crushing candy canes and infusing the dough with peppermint extract becomes a shared experience that fosters togetherness and bonding. The aroma of these cookies baking in the oven becomes a beacon, drawing loved ones together in anticipation of the awaited joyous treats.

Peppermint chocolate chip cookies find their place in the modern era as social media platforms become arenas for showcasing culinary creations. You may find many visually stunning images on Instagram, Pinterest, and other social media platforms that showcase the artistry of varieties of chocolate chip cookies with peppermint. Amateur and professional bakers share their recipes, techniques, and presentations, inspiring a global community of enthusiasts to embark on their culinary journeys. The digital age has transformed these cookies into not just edible delights but also subjects of creativity and admiration, fostering a sense of camaraderie among those who appreciate the intersection of culinary artistry and festive joy.

While creating peppermint chocolate chip cookies is a joyous and rewarding endeavor, it can also present challenges that demand attention to detail and precision. Achieving the right balance of peppermint flavor without overpowering the cookie's sweetness requires careful measurement of peppermint extract. Incorporating crushed candy canes into the dough necessitates finesse to ensure even distribution without creating an overly gritty texture. The potential for cookies to spread unevenly or for the peppermint chips to lose their vibrant color during baking poses additional considerations. However, in overcoming these challenges, bakers hone their skills and develop a deeper appreciation for the artistry of cookie making.

In conclusion, peppermint chocolate chip cookies are delectable ambassadors of holiday joy, infusing the season's spirit into every bite. From the aromatic anticipation of baking to the delightful textures and tastes that unfold with each bite, these cookies encapsulate the essence of festive indulgence. Whether enjoyed as standalone treats, incorporated into holiday desserts, or shared as tokens of affection, peppermint chocolate chip cookies become edible expressions of warmth, joy, and the timeless celebration of the holiday season.

CHAPTER IV

Creative Twists on Tradition

Cranberry orange shortbread cookies

With their delicate balance of sweet and tart flavors, Cranberry orange shortbread cookies emerge as a culinary masterpiece that captures the essence of the holiday season. The symphony of ingredients in these cookies— buttery shortbread, vibrant cranberries, and zesty orange— harmonizes to create a sensory experience that transcends mere indulgence. The journey begins with meticulously blending classic shortbread ingredients— butter, sugar, flour, and a pinch of salt—the festive flavors of orange and cranberry are used to this straightforward yet necessary foundation.

The infusion of orange zest into the shortbread dough becomes a transformative touch, elevating the cookies to citrusy brightness. As the zest melds with the buttery richness of the dough, it imparts a fragrant and nuanced citrus essence that plays a vital role in the overall flavor profile. The finely grated orange peel becomes a testament to the artistry in crafting these cookies, enhancing the taste and aroma that wafts through the kitchen as the cookies bake.

Cranberries add color and vibrancy to the shortbread with ruby-red hue and tart juiciness. Dried cranberries into the dough introduces pockets of tartness that counterbalances the sweetness of the shortbread. Each cranberry becomes a jewel nestled within the cookie, visually and gustatorily contributing to the overall composition. The careful distribution of these crimson gems ensures that every bite offers a delightful interplay of textures and tastes.

Shaping the shortbread dough into delicate rounds or festive shapes becomes a celebration of the artisanal nature of these cookies. Whether rolled into logs and sliced into rounds or pressed into molds that reflect the holiday spirit, the shaping process transforms the dough into individual works of edible art. The meticulous attention to detail pays homage to the tradition of shortbread craftsmanship while allowing for personal touches that reflect the creativity and spirit of the season.

Baking the cranberry orange shortbread cookies is a transformative stage in the culinary journey. The kitchen becomes an aromatic haven as the rich fragrance of butter and the citrusy notes of orange permeate the air. The cookies' golden edges and slightly crumbly texture emerge from the oven as embodiments of elegance and homely comfort. The careful balance of flavors, the visual appeal of cranberries embedded in each cookie, and the tender texture speak to the craftsmanship and artistry involved in creating these festive delights.

Cooling is crucial for the flavors to meld and the shortbread to set into its characteristic texture. The cranberries within each bite solidify as the cookies cool on wire racks, creating a delightful contrast to the buttery crumb. Patience during this stage receives compensation with cookies that not only boast a satisfying texture but also retain the freshness of the citrus and tartness of the cranberries.

The first bite into a cranberry orange shortbread cookie is a revelation of flavors that dance on the palate. The initial crunch gives way to a delicate crumble, releasing the rich buttery essence of the shortbread. The tartness of the cranberries provides a burst of brightness, while the lingering citrus notes from the orange zest leave a refreshing aftertaste. It's a symphony of sweet, tart, and citrusy notes that evoke the festive spirit and create a memorable gustatory experience.

Beyond their allure, cranberry orange shortbread cookies become versatile in holiday desserts. Crumbled into pie crusts, incorporated into trifle layers, or nestled into ice cream, these cookies infuse their distinctive flavors into various confections. The adaptability of cranberry orange shortbread extends to dessert bars, where crumbled shortbread becomes a delightful base for layers of cranberry compote or orange-infused custard. The creative possibilities unfold as bakers experiment with incorporating these cookies into a spectrum of sweet treats reflecting the festive holiday season.

The tradition of baking cranberry orange shortbread cookies aligns with the timeless customs of holiday festivities. Baking sessions, where families and friends come together to shape, bake, and enjoy these cookies, become cherished moments of shared joy and creativity. The aroma of butter, orange, and cranberries becomes a unifying thread that weaves through familial traditions, creating memories that endure from one holiday season to the next. Gifting a tin of cranberry orange shortbread expresses warmth and thoughtfulness, embodying the spirit of giving during the holidays.

In the contemporary landscape, the art of crafting cranberry orange shortbread cookies finds a new platform through social media. Platforms like Instagram and Pinterest showcase an array of visually stunning images that highlight the elegance and creativity of these cookies. Bakers share their recipes, techniques, and presentations, inspiring a global community of enthusiasts to embark on their culinary journeys. The digital age has transformed these cookies into not just delectable treats but also subjects of artistic expression, fostering a sense of camaraderie among those who appreciate the intersection of culinary artistry and festive joy.

Crafting cranberry orange shortbread cookies involves a joyful and rewarding endeavor but also challenges that demand precision and attention to detail. Achieving the right balance of sweetness and tartness requires carefully distributing cranberries and measuring sugar. Incorporating orange zest necessitates finesse to avoid bitterness while ensuring a robust citrus flavor. The potential for cookies to spread unevenly or for cranberries to become overly concentrated poses additional considerations. However, in navigating these challenges, bakers refine their skills and develop a deeper appreciation for the nuanced artistry of cookie making.

In conclusion, cranberry orange shortbread cookies are exquisite ambassadors of holiday indulgence, capturing the season's essence in every delicate bite. From the meticulous blending of buttery shortbread dough to the infusion of citrusy brightness and the burst of tartness from cranberries, each element contributes to the symphony of flavors and textures that define these cookies. Whether enjoyed as standalone treats, incorporated into holiday desserts, or shared as tokens of affection, cranberry orange shortbread cookies become edible expressions of warmth, joy, and the timeless celebration of the holiday season.

Pistachio and cardamom snowballs

Pistachio and cardamom snowballs, delicate spheres of delight, emerge as a fusion of exquisite flavors that transport the palate to an enchanting winter wonderland. These cookies, with their melt-in-your-mouth texture and a symphony of pistachio and cardamom notes, represent a culinary masterpiece that captures the spirit of the holiday season. The journey commences with the careful selection of high-quality pistachios, whose vibrant green hue and rich, nutty flavor lay the foundation for the unique character of these snowball cookies. The process involves grinding the pistachios into a fine powder, creating a base that imparts visual appeal and a subtle and luxurious nuttiness to the dough.

With its warm and citrusy undertones, Cardamom becomes the aromatic companion that elevates these snowballs to a realm of sophistication. The delicate fragrance of freshly ground cardamom infuses the dough, creating a fragrant embrace that mirrors the cozy ambiance of winter festivities. The careful balance of cardamom ensures that its presence is pronounced enough to be distinctive but subtle enough to harmonize with the overall flavor profile, contributing to the snowball's allure.

Creating the dough becomes a meditative process, where the precise combination of butter, sugar, flour, and the pistachio-cardamom blend sets the stage for the magic to unfold. The result is a dough that is rich buttery and infused with the essence of pistachios and the warmth of cardamom. Incorporating finely chopped pistachios into the dough adds a layer of texture, creating pockets of nuttiness that enhance the overall experience of these snowball cookies.

Shaping the dough into uniform rounds signifies the meticulous craftsmanship that defines pistachio and cardamom snowballs. Each portion is carefully measured and gently rolled between palms, creating petite spheres that promise a delicate crumble upon the first bite. The visual appeal of these snowballs lies not only in their uniformity but also in the vibrant green specks that hint at the pistachio bounty within. The shaping process becomes a ritual reflecting the intentionality and care invested in crafting these festive treats.

When the cookies release their alluring perfume, baking the pistachio and cardamom snowballs turns the kitchen into a fragrant haven. With their delicate golden color, the snowballs come out of the oven as evidence that the flavors and textures were precisely balanced. The air is filled with the enticing aroma of cardamom and pistachios, building to the moment. We'll relish these delectable treats.

A critical step in giving the snowballs their distinctive crumbly texture is cooling. As they cool on wire racks, a light dusting of powdered sugar becomes the finishing touch, resembling a dusting of snow on these edible confections. The sugar coating adds a visual elegance, transforming the cookies into winter-inspired delights, and contributes a subtle sweetness that complements pistachios' nuttiness and cardamom's warmth.

The first bite into a pistachio and cardamom snowball is a revelation of flavors that dance on the taste buds. The initial crunch gives way to a delicate crumble, releasing the rich buttery essence of the cookie. The finely ground and chopped pistachios create a symphony of textures—smooth and nutty from the ground pistachios and slightly crunchy from the chopped ones. With its citrusy notes, the cardamom adds a layer of complexity that lingers on the palate, inviting contemplation and appreciation of the carefully curated blend of flavors.

Beyond their allure, pistachio and cardamom snowballs become versatile companions in holiday desserts. These snowballs infuse their distinctive flavors into various confections, crumbled into pie crusts, folded into ice cream, or nestled alongside a scoop of pistachio or cardamom-flavored gelato. The creative possibilities extend to dessert bars, where crumbled snowballs become a delightful base for cream, custard, or fruit compote layers. The adaptability of pistachio and cardamom snowballs inspires culinary exploration, allowing bakers to experiment with incorporating these cookies into a spectrum of sweet treats that reflect the festive spirit.

The tradition of baking pistachio and cardamom snowballs aligns with the timeless customs of holiday festivities. Baking sessions, where families and friends come together to shape, bake, and enjoy these cookies, become cherished moments of shared joy and creativity. The aroma of pistachios and cardamom becomes a unifying thread that weaves through familial traditions, creating memories that endure from one holiday season to the next. Gifting a tin of pistachio and cardamom snowballs expresses warmth and thoughtfulness, embodying the spirit of giving during the holidays.

In the contemporary landscape, the art of crafting pistachio and cardamom snowballs finds a new platform through social media. Platforms like Instagram and Pinterest showcase an array of visually stunning images that highlight the elegance and creativity of these cookies. Bakers share their recipes, techniques, and presentations, inspiring a global community of enthusiasts to embark on their culinary journeys. The digital age has transformed these cookies into not just delectable treats but also subjects of artistic expression, fostering a sense of camaraderie among those who appreciate the intersection of culinary artistry and festive joy.

Crafting pistachio and cardamom snowballs involves a joyful and rewarding endeavor but also challenges that demand precision and attention to detail. Achieving the right balance of pistachio flavor without overwhelming the delicate nature of the cookie requires careful measurement and consideration. Incorporating cardamom requires finesse to ensure a nuanced presence that enhances rather than dominates the flavor profile. The potential for cookies to spread unevenly or for the powdered sugar coating to dissolve poses additional considerations. However, in navigating these challenges, bakers refine their skills and develop a deeper appreciation for the nuanced artistry of cookie making.

In conclusion, pistachio and cardamom snowballs are delicate ambassadors of holiday indulgence, capturing the season's essence in every nuanced bite. From the meticulous blending of buttery shortbread dough to the infusion of pistachio richness and the warmth of cardamom, each element contributes to the symphony of flavors and textures that define these cookies. Whether enjoyed as standalone treats, incorporated into holiday desserts, or shared as tokens of affection, pistachio and cardamom snowballs become edible expressions of warmth, joy, and the timeless celebration of the holiday season.

Chocolate-dipped almond biscotti

Chocolate-dipped almond biscotti, with their perfect marriage of crunch and richness, stand as timeless treasures in the world of baked delights. These elegant, double-baked Italian cookies are a testament to the artistry of biscuit-making, where simplicity and sophistication unite to create a treat that transcends seasons and cultures. The journey begins with selecting premium almonds, whose nutty essence forms the heart of these biscotti. Ground into a coarse meal, the almonds impart texture and flavor to the dough, establishing a foundation that promises a satisfying crunch in every bite.

Crafting chocolate-dipped almond biscotti unfolds with the meticulous blending of essential ingredients—flour, sugar, eggs, and baking powder. The almond meal becomes a harmonious addition, infusing the dough with a subtle nuttiness that enhances the overall depth of flavor. Forming the dough into logs and baking it until it becomes golden represents the first change from a soft, workable batter to the robust base of the biscotti. The seductive aroma of roasting almonds permeates the kitchen during this first baking, which also lays the foundation for the ultimate crisp texture.

The second act in the biscotti-making ballet involves slicing the partially baked logs into elegant, elongated pieces. This crucial step defines the classic form of biscotti, with its characteristic long shape and twice-baked nature. Return the sliced biscotti to the oven for a second bake to get the distinctive crunch that makes these cookies stand out. The color intensifies to a rich, deep brown, and the texture changes from a soft crumb to a crisp, gratifying bite, forming a canvas just waiting to be decorated with chocolate's richness.

Dipping each biscotti into a pool of molten chocolate becomes a transformative moment in the biscotti's journey. The rich, velvety embrace of dark, milk, or white chocolate adds a layer of indulgence that elevates these cookies to sheer decadence. Whether drizzled with artistic flair or enrobed to create a solid shell, the chocolate coating becomes the crowning touch that marries the rustic charm of almond-laden biscotti with the luxury of fine chocolate.

The cooling process is a compelling interlude, as the chocolate sets to form a glossy exterior that promises a luxurious mouthfeel. The biscotti, adorned in their chocolate finery, stand as edible jewels, ready to be savored as a standalone treat or with various beverages. The transition from a warm, pliable state to a firm, crisp texture completes the biscotti's metamorphosis, ensuring each bite delivers a symphony of flavors and textures.

The first bite into a chocolate-dipped almond biscotti is a revelation—a journey through layers of complexity that delight the senses. The initial crunch yields the firm yet yielding texture of the almond-studded crumb. The nuttiness of the almonds plays a delicate dance with the sweetness of the biscuit, creating a perfect balance that lingers on the palate. With its smooth richness, the chocolate adds a luxurious element, making a harmonious marriage of textures and tastes that epitomizes the artistry of biscotti.

Beyond their allure, chocolate-dipped almond biscotti become versatile companions in culinary creativity. The crunch of these cookies lends itself to a myriad of possibilities—crumbled into ice cream, incorporated into tiramisu, or paired with a creamy panna cotta. The adaptability of biscotti extends to dessert platters, where these cookies become elegant accompaniments to a selection of cheeses, fruits, and nuts. The creative possibilities unfurl as bakers experiment with incorporating chocolate-dipped almond biscotti into a

spectrum of sweet treats that celebrate the intersection of tradition and innovation.

The tradition of baking biscotti, rooted in Italian culture, transcends geographical boundaries, becoming a global culinary treasure. Crafting biscotti, whether in the warmth of a family kitchen or the ambiance of a bustling bakery, becomes a celebration of craftsmanship and tradition. Biscotti-making sessions, where generations come together to shape, bake, and enjoy these cookies, become cherished moments that weave the tapestry of familial traditions. Sharing a tin of chocolate-dipped almond biscotti expresses love and camaraderie, embodying the timeless joy of giving and receiving during festive occasions.

In the digital age, crafting chocolate-dipped almond biscotti finds a new canvas on social media platforms. Instagram, Pinterest, and other platforms showcase an array of visually stunning images that highlight the elegance and creativity of these cookies. Bakers share their recipes, techniques, and presentations, inspiring a global community of enthusiasts to embark on their biscotti-making journeys. The digital era has transformed these cookies into not just delectable treats but also subjects of artistic expression, fostering a sense of camaraderie among those who appreciate the intersection of culinary artistry and timeless tradition.

While crafting chocolate-dipped almond biscotti is a joyous and rewarding endeavor, it also presents challenges that demand attention to detail and precision. Achieving the right balance of almonds in the dough requires careful measurement and consideration of the almond meal's texture. Slicing the partially baked logs into precise pieces necessitates finesse to create uniform biscotti with an appealing visual consistency. Dipping the biscotti into chocolate requires a gentle touch to achieve an even coating that enhances aesthetics and taste—the potential for the chocolate to crack or the biscotti to crumble poses additional considerations. However, in

navigating these challenges, bakers refine their skills and develop a deeper appreciation for the nuanced artistry of biscotti making.

In conclusion, chocolate-dipped almond biscotti are epitomes of refined indulgence, capturing the essence of tradition and sophistication in every delicate bite. From the meticulous blending of almond-laden dough to the transformative moment of chocolate enrobing, each step in the biscotti-making process contributes to the symphony of flavors and textures that define these cookies. Whether enjoyed as standalone treats, paired with a cup of espresso, or incorporated into various desserts, chocolate-dipped almond biscotti become edible expressions of warmth, joy, and the timeless celebration of the holiday season.

Chapter V

International Flavors

German Lebkuchen

German Lebkuchen, a centuries-old confection steeped in tradition, emerges as a symbol of holiday festivities and the rich culinary heritage of Germany. Often referred to as gingerbread, Lebkuchen transcends a mere descriptor, embodying a complex amalgamation of spices, sweetness, and a storied past. The creation of Lebkuchen involves a meticulous blend of ingredients, each contributing to the symphony of flavors that define this festive treat. Ground almonds, honey, and an array of aromatic spices— cinnamon, cloves, nutmeg, and ginger— form the foundation of the dough, infusing it with a depth and complexity that elevates Lebkuchen to the realm of culinary art.

The dough-making process unfolds as a rhythmic dance, where precision is paramount to achieve the perfect balance of flavors. The ground almonds, with their nutty richness, add a distinctive texture while complementing the sweetness of honey. The spices, carefully measured and blended, become the heart of the dough, imparting warmth and complexity that resonate with the essence of the holiday season. The result is a dough that reflects not only the skill of the baker but also the cultural heritage embedded in every Lebkuchen.

Shaping the Lebkuchen dough is a celebration of artisanal craftsmanship. The dough is traditionally rolled and cut into various shapes, from hearts and stars to rounds and rectangles, each bearing the imprint of tradition and regional variations. The intricately shaped Lebkuchen enhances their visual appeal and contributes to the overall experience, with different shapes often associated with specific occasions, festivals, or regions within Germany. This step in the Lebkuchen-making process becomes a canvas for artistic expression, where bakers impart their individual touch while honoring a centuries-old tradition.

Baking the Lebkuchen is a transformative stage where the kitchen becomes a fragrant haven, redolent with the heady aroma of spices. The Lebkuchen, with their golden-brown hue and enticing fragrance, emerge from the oven as testaments to the alchemical magic of baking. Cooling is crucial, allowing the flavors to meld and the Lebkuchen to achieve their characteristic chewy texture. Some variations, particularly those from Nuremberg, undergo an additional step of glazing with a sugar or chocolate coating, adding a layer of sweetness that enhances the overall indulgence.

The first bite into a piece of Lebkuchen is a sensory journey that encapsulates the essence of the holiday season. The initial resistance gives way to a chewy and tender interior, where the ground almonds create a melange of textures. The harmoniously blended spices offer a symphony of flavors that dance on the taste buds—warm cinnamon, aromatic cloves, the zing of ginger, and the subtle allure of nutmeg. The sweetness of honey, the unifying element in the dough, adds a layer of complexity, making each bite a nuanced experience that lingers on the palate.

Beyond their appeal, Lebkuchen serves as cultural ambassadors, embodying the festive customs and regional variations within Germany. The city of Nuremberg, renowned for its Lebkuchen, holds a special place in the hearts of enthusiasts. The Nuremberg Lebkuchen, distinguished by their small size and distinct shapes, enjoy protected geographical indication status, underscoring their significance in German culinary heritage. The Lebkuchenmarkt (Lebkuchen market) in Nuremberg, held during the Christmas season, has become a pilgrimage site for those seeking the authentic taste of this iconic treat.

The tradition of gifting Lebkuchen during the holidays extends beyond Germany's borders, as these delectable treats become sought-after symbols of warmth and goodwill. Packaged in ornate tins or adorned with festive ribbons, Lebkuchen become tokens of affection exchanged between friends and family. Presenting a box of Lebkuchen becomes an expression of thoughtfulness and a shared celebration of the season.

In the modern era, the allure of Lebkuchen extends globally, finding new avenues of appreciation and adaptation. By sharing their culinary heritage, German immigrants introduce Lebkuchen to diverse communities worldwide. The classic Lebkuchen recipe becomes a canvas for creative interpretations, inspiring bakers to experiment with variations incorporating local ingredients or catering to specific dietary preferences. Social media platforms, especially during the holiday season, showcase the artistry and creativity of Lebkuchen enthusiasts, fostering a global community that appreciates and celebrates this iconic treat.

While creating Lebkuchen is a labor of love, it has its challenges. Skill and talent are required to balance the spice, roll the dough to the ideal thickness, and perfect the glazing or decorating techniques. The traditional nature of Lebkuchen-making, with its reliance on quality ingredients and time-honored techniques, underscores the importance of patience and attention to detail. The challenges, however, become part of the journey, adding to the satisfaction of creating a treat that not only tantalizes the taste buds but also carries the weight of cultural significance.

In conclusion, German Lebkuchen represents more than a confection; it encapsulates a rich tapestry of tradition, craftsmanship, and festive spirit. From the aromatic blend of spices to the artisanal shaping and the transformative magic of baking, each step in the Lebkuchen-making process contributes to a culinary symphony that transcends generations. Whether enjoyed as a symbol of German holiday traditions, a cherished gift, or a creative adaptation in global kitchens, Lebkuchen embodies the essence of the holiday season—a time for warmth, celebration, and the joyous sharing of culinary heritage.

Italian pizzelle

Italian pizzelle, delicate waffle-like cookies with intricate patterns, emerge as a culinary treasure that weaves together the flavors of tradition, craftsmanship, and familial heritage. Originating from Italy's heart, particularly Abruzzo and Molise's regions, pizzelle holds a unique place in the pantheon of Italian sweets. Creating a pizzle involves combining flour, eggs, sugar, and butter. Still, the finesse in preparation and the artistry of the iron mold elevate these cookies to a status of culinary art.

The batter becomes the vehicle through which the essence of pizzelle is expressed; it is similar to a thin pancake batter. The blending of ingredients is a ritual, often passed down through generations, where the proportions and nuances of mixing become a family secret. Depending on regional preferences, the gentle fragrance of vanilla or anise adds a subtle aromatic note, infusing the batter with a scent that speaks to the comfort of home and the anticipation of indulgence.

The heart of the pizzelle-making process lies in using a specialized iron mold known as a pizzelle press. This press, often adorned with intricate designs, imparts the characteristic patterns that make each pizzella a work of edible art. The process requires a delicate balance of heat and timing, with the batter poured onto the heated iron and quickly pressed into shape before it sets. The result is a thin, crisp cookie adorned with a symmetrical design, reflecting the meticulous craftsmanship involved in its creation.

Baking pizzelle becomes a sensory experience as the aroma of the batter transforms into the scent of freshly baked cookies. Depending on the chosen flavor profile, the kitchen becomes an aromatic haven filled with the fragrance of vanilla or anise. The cookies, with their golden hue and intricate patterns, emerge from the press as edible masterpieces that pay homage to the artistry and tradition of Italian baking. The cooling process is a crucial stage where the pizzelle achieves its characteristic crisp texture, setting the stage for the moment of indulgence.

The first bite into a pizzella is a revelation of textures and flavors—a harmony of crispness and tenderness. The delicate lace-like patterns give way to a satisfying crunch, while the flavor profile unfolds with the subtle sweetness of the batter and the aromatic notes of vanilla or anise. The simplicity of the ingredients belies the complexity of the taste, creating a treat that is both comforting and sophisticated. Whether enjoyed on its own or paired with a cup of espresso, pizzelle becomes a culinary bliss that transcends the ordinary.

Beyond its appeal, pies are now a staple of Italian cooking customs and family get-togethers. These cookies, often made during special occasions like weddings, anniversaries, or religious festivals, carry the weight of shared memories and generations of hands shaping the batter. Making pizzelle becomes a familial ritual when generations come together to pass down the recipe, artistry, and tradition of creating these beloved treats.

The regional variations of pizzelle reflect the diverse culinary landscape of Italy. In Abruzzo, anise is prevalent, imparting a distinctive licorice-like flavor to the cookies. In Molise, vanilla takes center stage, offering a milder and more universally appealing taste. The choice of flavor, along with variations in the thickness of the batter and the intricacy of the iron mold patterns, becomes a source of regional pride and identity. Pizzelle-making competitions, where bakers showcase their skill and creativity, further underscore the significance of these cookies in Italy's cultural tapestry.

The tradition of gifting pizzelle extends beyond familial circles, as these delicate cookies become tokens of affection shared with friends and neighbors. Whether packaged in decorative tins or presented on festive platters, pizzelle become edible expressions of warmth and goodwill. Receiving a box of pizzelle becomes a cherished moment, evoking a sense of connection to tradition and the giver's generosity.

In the modern era, the allure of pizzelle extends beyond Italy's borders, finding resonance in diverse culinary landscapes. Italian immigrants, carrying their culinary heritage, introduce pizzelle to new communities, where these cookies become symbols of cultural exchange and appreciation. The classic pizzelle recipe becomes a canvas for creative adaptations, inspiring bakers to experiment with flavors, shapes, and even gluten-free or vegan variations. Social media platforms become vibrant spaces where pizzelle enthusiasts share their creations, fostering a global community that celebrates the artistry and joy of pizzelle-making.

While creating pizzelle is characterized by simplicity, it has challenges. Achieving the right balance of ingredients and mastering the timing and technique of pressing the batter onto the iron mold demand practice and finesse. The potential for overcooking or undercooking, leading to a loss of delicate crispness or an imbalance in flavors, requires a keen eye and attentive hands. Making pizzelle becomes a lesson in precision and intuition, where the baker refines their skills with each batch, striving for that perfect combination of texture and taste.

In conclusion, Italian pizzelle represents more than a cookie—they embody a cultural legacy, a familial tradition, and the artistry of simplicity. From blending essential ingredients to the artful pressing on iron molds, each step in the pizzelle-making process is a testament to the culinary heritage of Italy. Whether enjoyed during festive occasions, shared among loved ones, or adapted and appreciated in kitchens worldwide, pizzelle become a timeless celebration of tradition, craftsmanship, and the joy of creating something beautiful and delicious.

French sablés

French sablés, delicate and crumbly shortbread cookies, stand as a testament to the refined artistry of French pastry making. Hailing from the rich culinary tradition of France, sablés derive their name from the French word "sable," meaning sand—a nod to the tender, sandy texture that distinguishes these treats. The creation of sablés involves a harmonious interplay of classic ingredients: butter, sugar, flour, and a touch of salt. However, the precision in combining these elements and the emphasis on quality elevate sablés to a level of sophistication and epitomize French patisserie.

The butter, often of high quality and with a rich fat content, becomes the backbone of sablés, imparting not only richness but also the distinct crumbly texture that is the hallmark of these cookies. The sugar, whether granulated or powdered, contributes sweetness and aids in the delicate balance of flavors. The flour, carefully measured and sifted, becomes the binding agent, creating a pliable dough that yields the desired tender crumb. A pinch of salt adds a subtle contrast, heightening the overall taste and allowing the sweetness to be nuanced.

The dough-making process unfolds with an emphasis on finesse and restraint. The butter is often creamed with sugar until light and fluffy, creating a base as the canvas for the delicate flavors to unfold. The incorporation of flour is gradual, avoiding overmixing to prevent the development of gluten and ensuring the tender, crumbly texture that defines sablés. The resulting dough is a testament to the French pastry-making approach—simple yet precise, emphasizing quality ingredients and meticulous technique.

Shaping the sablés expresses the baker's artistry, where the dough is carefully portioned and formed into various shapes. Traditional forms include rounds, squares, or rectangles, while creative bakers may use molds or cookie cutters to craft intricate designs. The shaping process becomes a celebration of individuality within the confines of a classic French recipe, where each sablé is a unique expression of the baker's touch. The gentle imprint of a fork or the adornment with slivered almonds further adds to the visual appeal, creating cookies that are as beautiful as they are delicious.

Baking the sablés transforms the kitchen into a fragrant sanctuary, as the rich aroma of butter and sugar fills the air. The cookies, with golden edges and pale centers, emerge from the oven as golden treasures that beckon with the promise of indulgence. The cooling process is crucial, allowing the sablés to set into their characteristic crumbly texture. The fragility of the cookies becomes a testament to their quality and craftsmanship, with each bite offering a symphony of textures and flavors.

The first bite into a sablé is an exquisite experience—a journey through layers of crumbly tenderness and buttery richness. The delicacy of the texture gives way to a subtle sweetness that is neither cloying nor overpowering. The butter imparts a luxurious mouthfeel with its high-fat content, creating a moment of pure indulgence. The sablé, often enjoyed with a cup of tea or coffee, becomes a pause in the day—a moment to savor the refined simplicity of French pastry.

Beyond their allure, sablés are embedded in the cultural tapestry of French culinary traditions. With their delicate elegance, these cookies are often associated with special occasions, afternoon tea, or holiday festivities. Making sablés, whether in a family kitchen or a professional bakery, becomes a celebration of craftsmanship and a nod to the timeless appeal of French pastry making. Sablés are not just cookies; they are edible expressions of a culinary heritage that values precision, quality, and the pursuit of pleasure in simple yet exquisite pleasures.

The regional variations of sablés reflect the diversity within French patisserie. In Brittany, sablés often incorporate ground almonds or hazelnuts, adding a nutty richness to the traditional recipe. In Provence, including citrus zest or a hint of lavender offers a nod to the region's sun-soaked flavors. The variations extend to the shapes and sizes, with some areas favoring larger, heart-shaped sablés while others embrace dainty, bite-sized versions. The variety seen in the world of sablés shows how versatile French pastry creation is, as local ingredients and culinary customs are honored.

The tradition of sharing sablés extends beyond familial circles, as these cookies become tokens of appreciation and hospitality. Whether presented in ornate tins, wrapped with ribbons, or arranged on delicate platters, sablés become edible gifts that convey thoughtfulness and sophistication. Offering a plate of sablés becomes a gesture of warmth and hospitality, a shared moment of pleasure transcending language and cultural boundaries.

In the modern era, the allure of sablés extends globally, finding appreciation in kitchens worldwide. French culinary influence, facilitated by cookbooks, culinary classes, and digital media, introduces sablés to new audiences eager to experience the refinement of French pastry making. The classic sablé recipe becomes a canvas for creative adaptations, inspiring bakers to experiment with flavor infusions, glazes, or even sandwiching them with decadent fillings. Social media platforms become vibrant spaces where sablé enthusiasts share their creations, fostering a global community that appreciates the artistry and joy of sablé-making.

Although making sablés is a simple process, it requires a careful understanding of materials and methods. Achieving the delicate balance of tenderness and crumbliness requires precision in measuring and handling the dough. The potential for overmixing, leading to a stricter texture, or underbaking, resulting in a lack of crispness, necessitates a discerning eye and experienced hands. Making sablés becomes a lesson in patience and the art of restraint, where the pursuit of perfection lies in mastering the fundamentals.

In conclusion, French sablés represent more than a cookie—they embody the essence of French patisserie, a celebration of refined simplicity and the pursuit of pleasure in culinary craftsmanship. From the precise blending of ingredients to the artful shaping and the transformative magic of baking, each step in the sablé-making process reflects the French culinary ethos. Whether enjoyed during special occasions, shared among loved ones, or adapted and appreciated in kitchens worldwide, sablés become a timeless celebration of tradition, craftsmanship, and the joy of creating something exquisite and delightful.

Chapter VI

Gluten-Free and Vegan Options

Almond flour snowball cookies

Almond flour snowball cookies, delicate and crumbly, present a delightful twist to the classic snowball cookie recipe. These almond flour snowballs combine the festive appeal of traditional snowball cookies with the richness of almonds, resulting from the growing popularity of gluten-free options and the desire for a healthier treat. Almond flour, made from finely ground blanched almonds, introduces a nutty richness and a delicate texture that sets these cookies apart. The creation of almond flour snowballs unfolds as a celebration of simplicity and quality ingredients, emphasizing the natural flavors of almonds while offering a gluten-free option for those with dietary preferences or restrictions.

The heart of almond flour snowballs lies in the almond flour itself—an ingredient that adds nutritional value and a distinctive flavor profile. With their natural oils and nuttiness, the almonds create a flour that contributes a subtle richness and moisture to the cookie dough. The almond flour becomes the canvas on which the other classic snowball ingredients—butter, powdered sugar, and vanilla—work their magic. The result is a dough that is both tender and crumbly, capturing the essence of traditional snowball cookies while offering a unique almond-infused experience. The process of making almond flour snowballs follows the familiar ritual of cookie-making, emphasizing the quality of ingredients.

The almond flour is often combined with softened butter, creating a base that forms the backbone of the cookies. For sweetness, powdered sugar is added, and vanilla essence adds its olfactory appeal. The ingredients are combined with care so as not to overwork the dough. The resulting dough, which promises to make wonderful snowball cookies with almond flavor, is a monument to the alchemy of baking.

Shaping the almond flour snowballs becomes a tactile experience as bakers gently form the dough into bite-sized rounds. The cookies, reminiscent of snow-covered mountains, are often rolled in powdered sugar before baking, creating a sweet and snowy exterior. The shaping process is not just a step in the recipe; it becomes a moment of connection with the tradition of snowball cookies—a tradition that dates back generations and spans various cultures. The gentle imprint left by the baker's hands on each cookie adds a personal touch, making every almond flour snowball unique.

Baking these cookies transforms the kitchen into a fragrant sanctuary as the almond-rich aroma wafts through the air. The almond flour snowballs, with their pale exteriors, emerge from the oven as golden delights that embody the festive spirit. The cooling process is crucial, allowing the cookies to set into their characteristic crumbly texture. The final dusting of powdered sugar becomes a finishing touch, creating a snowy veil that adds sweetness and visual appeal. The fragility of these cookies becomes part of their charm, promising a delicate yet satisfying bite.

The first bite into an almond flour snowball is a revelation of textures and flavors—an interplay of tenderness and nutty richness. The crumbly exterior gives way to a melt-in-the-mouth experience, where the almond flour imparts its distinct flavor. The sweetness of the powdered sugar provides a perfect counterpoint, creating a harmonious balance that lingers on the palate.

The almond flour snowball enjoyed with a cup of tea or coffee becomes a moment of cozy indulgence—a treat that encapsulates the joy of the holiday season.

Beyond their appeal, snowballs made with almond flour pay homage to the changing face of baking, wherever dietary restrictions and alternative flours are welcomed. Because they are gluten-free, these cookies can satisfy various tastes and preferences. Almond flour, celebrated for its nutritional benefits and versatility, becomes a hero ingredient that elevates the cookies beyond a mere adaptation. The almond flour snowball cookies symbolize inclusivity, allowing individuals with gluten sensitivities to partake in the joy of festive baking.

The tradition of sharing almond flour snowballs extends beyond dietary considerations, as these cookies become tokens of warmth and hospitality. Whether arranged on a festive platter, packaged in decorative boxes, or shared in a cookie exchange, almond flour snowballs symbolize thoughtfulness and shared joy. Presenting a plate of these gluten-free delights becomes a gesture of inclusion, offering a sweet treat that caters to various tastes without compromising flavor or texture.

In the modern era, the allure of almond flour snowballs extends beyond the kitchen, finding resonance in the digital realm. Social media platforms become vibrant spaces where bakers and enthusiasts share their adaptations, creative presentations, and personal experiences with almond flour snowball cookies. The online community becomes a source of inspiration, fostering a global network of individuals who appreciate the artistry and joy of gluten-free baking.

With their visual appeal and distinctive flavor, Almond flour snowballs become stars in the virtual world, enticing others to join the festive baking festivities. While creating almond flour snowballs is simple, it has challenges. Achieving the right balance of ingredients, ensuring proper shaping, and mastering the delicate nature of the dough demands a careful hand and an understanding of the nuances of almond flour. The potential for the cookies to crumble or lose shape poses considerations that require attention to detail. However, it's in navigating these challenges that bakers refine their skills and develop a deeper appreciation for the artistry of gluten- free baking.

In conclusion, almond flour snowball cookies represent more than a gluten-free adaptation—they embody the spirit of innovation, inclusivity, and the joy of festive baking. From the incorporation of almond flour to the shaping and transformative magic of baking, each step in the process reflects the evolving landscape of contemporary baking.

Whether enjoyed by those with gluten sensitivities or embraced by a wider audience seeking a unique twist on a classic, almond flour snowballs become a timeless celebration of tradition, craftsmanship, and the delight of creating something both delectable and accommodating.

Vegan gingerbread men

Vegan gingerbread men, an innovative take on a classic holiday treat, stand at the intersection of tradition and modern dietary preferences.

These plant-based cookies, crafted without animal products, showcase the versatility and creativity inherent in vegan baking while capturing the nostalgic charm of traditional gingerbread.
The essence of vegan gingerbread men lies in omitting ingredients like butter, eggs, and milk, replacing them with plant-based alternatives that yield a deliciously spiced and cruelty-free cookie.
Creating these vegan delights is a testament to the evolving landscape of culinary choices, where individuals seek treats that align with their ethical values without compromising on taste.

At the heart of vegan gingerbread men is the thoughtful selection of plant-based ingredients that mimic conventional gingerbread's traditional flavors and textures. Vegan butter, often made from oils like coconut or avocado, takes the place of dairy butter, ensuring a rich and creamy base for the cookie dough. Plant-based milk, whether almond, soy, or oat, contributes the necessary moisture, while molasses adds a deep, caramel-like sweetness quintessential to gingerbread. Flour, sugar, and a medley of spices—cinnamon, ginger, cloves, and nutmeg—form the backbone of the dough, infusing it with the warm and aromatic notes that define this festive treat.

The process of making vegan gingerbread men mirrors the traditional approach, with a focus on plant-based substitutions and mindful choices.

The vegan butter is creamed with sugar until light and fluffy, creating a foundation that emulates the texture of conventional gingerbread. Molasses are added, providing sweetness and the characteristic dark color distinguishing gingerbread. The spices are carefully measured and blended into the dough, creating a fragrant mixture that promises the familiar warmth associated with gingerbread cookies.

Shaping the vegan gingerbread men is a tactile experience, as bakers cut out familiar shapes with cookie cutters, creating representations of festive characters. Using gingerbread men's bodies connects the vegan adaptation with the timeless tradition of decorating and enjoying gingerbread during the holiday season.

The careful placement of raisins or vegan chocolate chips for eyes and buttons adds a whimsical touch, bringing these plant-based cookies to life with personality and charm. The shaping process celebrates tradition and individual creativity within vegan baking.

Baking the vegan gingerbread men transforms the kitchen into a fragrant haven, as the warm spices mingle with the sweet aroma of molasses.

With their golden-brown edges and slightly chewy

centers, the cookies emerge from the oven as delectable vegan counterparts to the classic gingerbread. The cooling process is crucial, allowing the cookies to set into the desired texture—a delicate balance between firmness and tenderness.

The final step often involves decorating the cooled

gingerbread men with vegan icing, creating intricate designs, or adding a festive flair that elevates their visual appeal.

The first bite into a vegan gingerbread man is a

celebration of flavors and textures—a harmonious blend of sweet, spicy, and chewy. The plant-based ingredients work in tandem to recreate the familiar taste of traditional gingerbread, with the spices dancing on the palate and the molasses offering a rich undertone. The absence of dairy or eggs does not compromise the indulgent experience; instead, it showcases the ingenuity of vegan baking in crafting ethical and delightful treats. Enjoyed with a cup of dairy-free cocoa or a spiced almond milk latte, vegan gingerbread men become a festive indulgence that transcends dietary choices.

Beyond their allure, vegan gingerbread men represent a

conscious shift towards more compassionate and sustainable culinary practices. As the demand for plant-based options continues to rise, these cookies become ambassadors of a lifestyle that seeks to minimize the ecological footprint while promoting animal welfare. Vegan baking, once considered a niche endeavor, has become a mainstream culinary movement, embraced by individuals who view their dietary choices as a reflection of their values and a commitment to a more compassionate world.

The tradition of gifting or sharing vegan gingerbread men extends beyond the boundaries of vegan communities, as these cookies become bridges of understanding and inclusivity. Whether presented on a festive platter, tucked into gift boxes adorned with vegan ribbons, or shared in cookie exchanges, vegan gingerbread men become symbols of thoughtfulness and culinary innovation. Offering a plate of these plant-based delights becomes an invitation to partake in a festive tradition that accommodates diverse dietary preferences.

In the modern era, the allure of vegan gingerbread men extends far beyond the kitchen, finding resonance in the digital realm. Social media platforms become vibrant spaces where vegan bakers and enthusiasts share their adaptations, creative presentations, and personal experiences with vegan gingerbread. The online community becomes a source of inspiration, fostering a global network of individuals who appreciate the artistry and joy of plant-based baking. Vegan gingerbread men, with their visual appeal and ethical foundation, become stars in the virtual world, enticing others to join the festive celebration of compassionate and flavorful treats.

While thoughtful substitutions mark the process of creating vegan gingerbread men, it is not without its challenges. Achieving the right balance of flavors and textures without using traditional ingredients demands a nuanced understanding of plant-based alternatives. The potential for vegan butter to behave differently in the dough or for plant-based milk to introduce varying moisture levels requires adaptability and experimentation. Creating vegan gingerbread men becomes a journey of discovery, where bakers refine their skills and contribute to the growing repertoire of delicious and cruelty-free desserts.

In conclusion, vegan gingerbread men represent more than a plant-based adaptation of a classic—they embody the spirit of culinary innovation, compassion, and the joy of festive baking. Each step in the process reflects the evolution of modern dietary preferences, from the selection of plant-based ingredients to the shaping and transformative magic of baking. Whether enjoyed by those with vegan lifestyles or embraced by a wider audience seeking a delicious and ethical treat, vegan gingerbread men become a timeless celebration of tradition, creativity, and the delight of creating something heartwarming and cruelty-free.

Gluten-free peppermint brownie bites

Gluten-free peppermint brownie bites, a delightful confluence of rich chocolate, refreshing peppermint, and the absence of gluten represent a harmonious marriage of decadence and dietary inclusivity. These bite-sized treats, crafted for those with gluten sensitivities or those choosing a gluten-free lifestyle, reimagine the classic brownie in a way that not only caters to diverse dietary needs but also tantalizes the taste buds with the festive allure of peppermint.

The creation of gluten-free peppermint brownie bites

becomes a testament to the evolving landscape of baking, where the pursuit of flavor and texture intersects with the demand for inclusive treats that a broad audience can enjoy.

The heart of gluten-free peppermint brownie bites lies in

the meticulous selection of gluten-free ingredients that contribute to traditional brownies' rich and fudgy texture. Gluten-free flour, often a blend of rice flour, tapioca starch, and potato starch, replaces conventional wheat flour to ensure a safe option for those with gluten sensitivities. Cocoa powder, a staple in brownie recipes, adds a deep chocolatey flavor, while gluten-free baking powder or baking soda helps the brownie bites achieve the desired rise and tenderness. The gluten-free peppermint extract infuses the brownies with peppermint's excellent and refreshing essence, creating a perfect balance of flavors.

The process of making gluten-free peppermint brownie bites follows the familiar ritual of brownie-making, emphasizing gluten-free substitutions. The gluten-free flour is combined with cocoa powder, sugar, and a pinch of salt, creating a dry mixture that forms the backbone of the brownie bites. Eggs, or suitable egg replacements for a vegan adaptation, contribute to the fudgy texture, while melted chocolate and butter provide the necessary richness. Peppermint extract becomes the show's star, adding a festive twist to the brownie bites and infusing them with the unmistakable aroma of the holiday season.

Shaping gluten-free peppermint brownie bites becomes a tactile experience as bakers carefully spoon or scoop portions of the brownie batter onto baking sheets. Using mini muffin tins or silicone molds ensures uniformity in size, creating bite-sized indulgences that are visually appealing and easy to handle. The shaping process becomes a celebration of individual creativity, as some may choose to incorporate gluten-free peppermint candy pieces for added texture or drizzle the baked brownie bites with dairy-free chocolate for an extra layer of decadence. Baking these brownie bites transforms the kitchen into a fragrant sanctuary as the rich aroma of chocolate and peppermint mingles in the air.

The gluten-free peppermint brownie bites, glossy tops, and slightly cracked surfaces emerge from the oven as miniature delights that bring flavor to every taste. The cooling process is essential, allowing the brownie bites to set into the desired fudgy texture while preserving the freshness of the peppermint flavor. The final dusting of powdered sugar or a sprinkle of crushed peppermint candy becomes a festive touch, enhancing the visual appeal and adding extra sweetness.

The first bite into a gluten-free peppermint brownie bite is a sensory journey—a dance of textures and flavors that encapsulates the essence of the holiday season. The fudgy interior, studded with the occasional crunch of peppermint candy, melts in the mouth, offering a moment of indulgence that defies the constraints of gluten-free baking. The marriage of rich chocolate and refreshing peppermint creates a symphony of comforting and festive tastes, making these brownie bites a perfect addition to holiday gatherings or a cozy evening by the fireplace.

Beyond their allure, gluten-free peppermint brownie bites symbolize a shift in baking culture—a move towards inclusivity and acknowledging that dietary restrictions should not limit the enjoyment of indulgent treats. As gluten-free living becomes more prevalent, these brownie bites become ambassadors of a culinary movement that seeks to provide options without compromising taste or quality. The demand for gluten-free alternatives extends beyond those with sensitivities as more individuals explore diverse dietary choices in pursuit of healthier and more inclusive lifestyles.

The tradition of sharing gluten-free peppermint brownie bites extends beyond gluten-free communities, as these treats become bridges between dietary preferences. Whether arranged on a festive platter, in gift boxes adorned with gluten-free ribbons or shared in holiday gatherings, gluten-free peppermint brownie bites become symbols of thoughtfulness and culinary innovation. Offering a plate of these inclusive delights invites you to savor the festive season without concern for gluten-related restrictions. In the modern era, the allure of gluten-free peppermint brownie bites extends far beyond the kitchen, finding resonance in the digital realm. Social media platforms become vibrant spaces where bakers and enthusiasts share their adaptations, creative presentations, and personal experiences with gluten-free baking. The online community becomes a source of inspiration, fostering a global network of individuals who appreciate the artistry and joy of gluten-free treats. Gluten-free peppermint brownie bites, with their visual appeal and inclusive nature, have become stars in the virtual world, enticing others to join the celebration of flavorful and accessible desserts. While creating gluten-free peppermint brownie bites demands careful consideration of ingredients, it is not without its rewards.

Achieving the right balance of fudginess, chocolate richness, and peppermint freshness requires a discerning palate and an understanding of gluten-free baking dynamics. The potential for gluten-free flour blends to behave differently poses considerations that demand adaptability and experimentation. Creating gluten-free peppermint brownie bites becomes a journey of discovery, where bakers contribute to the growing repertoire of delicious and inclusive desserts.

In conclusion, gluten-free peppermint brownie bites represent more than a gluten-free adaptation—they embody the spirit of culinary innovation, inclusivity, and the joy of festive baking. From the careful selection of gluten-free ingredients to the shaping and transformative magic of baking, each step in the process reflects the evolution of modern dietary preferences. Whether enjoyed by those with gluten sensitivities or embraced by a wider audience seeking a delicious and inclusive treat, gluten-free peppermint brownie bites become a timeless celebration of tradition, creativity, and the delight of creating something both indulgent and accessible.

CHAPTER VII

Gift-Worthy Treats

Packaging ideas for holiday cookies

Packaging ideas for holiday cookies transform sharing sweet treats into a festive and visually appealing experience. As the holiday season approaches, the joy of baking extends beyond the kitchen to the art of presentation, creating a visual feast that enhances the gift-giving tradition. The packaging reflects thoughtfulness and creativity, turning a simple batch of cookies into a delightful token of warmth and goodwill.

One charming and classic packaging option for holiday cookies is the decorative tin or cookie tin. Containers come in various sizes, shapes, and designs, offering a timeless vessel for an assortment of cookies. From vintage-inspired cans adorned with holiday motifs to modern, sleek designs, these containers protect the cookies and add nostalgia to the gift. Because Tins can be recycled, the present giver can enjoy the container long after consuming the cookies. Line them with parchment or colorful tissue paper for an extra bit of elegance.

Another popular and customizable packaging idea is the festive cookie box. Cookie boxes can be crafted from cardboard or paper, offering a canvas for creativity. Bakers can personalize the boxes with holiday-themed stickers, stamps, or illustrations. A transparent window on the package provides a sneak peek of the delicious contents, adding to the anticipation. To enhance the holiday spirit, consider choosing boxes in colors like red, green, or white and tying them with ribbons or twine for a finishing touch.

For a touch of rustic charm, mason jars make an excellent choice for packaging holiday cookies. These transparent containers allow the recipient to see the layers of cookies, creating a visually appealing presentation. To add a festive flair, layer different types of cookies or create a colorful mix of shapes and sizes. Tie a piece of gingham or holiday-themed fabric around the lid, securing it with twine or ribbon for a cozy and homespun look. Mason jars showcase the cookies and provide an airtight seal to keep them fresh.

Bags with personalized labels offer a versatile and budget-friendly packaging option. Clear cellophane bags allow the vibrant colors and shapes of the cookies to shine through, creating an eye-catching display. Personalized labels can include holiday greetings, the name of the cookie, or a heartfelt message, adding a thoughtful touch to the presentation. Tie the bags with festive ribbons or twine, and consider including a small holiday ornament or tag for an extra touch of charm.

For a whimsical and eco-friendly option, consider using reusable cloth bags. Cloth bags can be made from festive fabrics and tied with ribbons or twine. Not only are these bags environmentally conscious, but they also offer a charming and rustic aesthetic. Add a sprig of evergreen or a cinnamon stick to the tie to further enhance the presentation. Cloth bags are an excellent way to share holiday cookies and a sustainable choice that aligns with the season's spirit.

Creating a thematic and festive cookie basket adds a touch of luxury to holiday gifting. Bakers can select a beautiful basket or woven tray and arrange an assortment of cookies. Incorporate holiday-themed napkins, ornaments, or small decorations to elevate the presentation. Use festive cupcake liners or mini cupcake wrappers between layers to keep the cookies fresh and secure. A finishing touch of cellophane wrap and a festive bow completes the ensemble, turning the cookie basket into a memorable gift.

In the digital age, sending virtual cookies has become a creative and fun way to share the joy of holiday baking. Virtual cookies involve creating an e-card or digital image of a beautifully decorated cookie and a heartfelt message. Bakers can use graphic design tools to add personal touches such as frosting details, sprinkles, or holiday backgrounds. The digital image can then be shared through email, social media, or messaging apps, allowing for a unique and contactless way to spread holiday cheer to friends and loved ones nearby.

A playful and edible packaging idea involves incorporating cookies into a festive wreath. Bakers can arrange different types of cookies in a circular pattern, creating a visually stunning wreath. The cookies can be individually wrapped or attached with ribbons to maintain shape. This creative presentation showcases the cookies and is a beautiful centerpiece or decoration. Incorporate decorative elements like holly leaves, berries, or edible gold or silver dust to add a layer of holiday magic.

For those who enjoy a touch of elegance, consider presenting cookies in glass or acrylic containers. Clear containers provide a sophisticated display, allowing the colors and textures of the cookies to take center stage. Layering different shapes or stacking cookies in an organized pattern creates a visually pleasing arrangement. Tie a satin ribbon or velvet bow around the container for a luxurious finishing touch. Glass or acrylic containers showcase the cookies and make for a stunning and reusable gift.

In conclusion, packaging holiday cookies involves more than mere presentation—it becomes an art form that enhances the joy of giving and receiving. Whether opting for classic tins, charming boxes, rustic mason jars, reusable cloth bags, thematic baskets, virtual cookies, edible wreaths, or elegant glass containers, the packaging becomes an integral part of the festive experience. The choice of packaging reflects the thoughtfulness, creativity, and care invested in sharing the delightful tradition of holiday baking. As the holiday season unfolds, presenting cookies in these thoughtfully chosen packages transforms a simple gesture into a cherished and festive celebration of warmth, love, and deliciousness.

Tips for shipping cookies

Shipping cookies, especially during the holiday season, requires careful consideration and strategic planning to ensure that the sweet treats arrive at their destination in perfect condition. Whether sending homemade cookies to loved ones, participating in a cookie exchange, or running a small baking business, following a set of tips can make the shipping process smoother and maintain the quality of the cookies.

First and foremost, choosing the appropriate cookies for delivery is essential. Cookies differ in their ability to withstand changes in temperature during transportation. Sturdy cookies with a lower moisture content, such as shortbread, biscotti, or gingerbread, tend to fare better in shipping than delicate or moist cookies like meringues or frosted varieties. Choosing cookies that can withstand handling and temperature fluctuations is the first step in ensuring a successful shipping experience.

Once the appropriate cookies are selected, the next consideration is the packaging. Packaging is vital in protecting cookies from breakage and maintaining their freshness. Individually wrapping or sealing cookies in airtight packaging helps prevent them from drying out or absorbing odors during transit. Placing sheets of parchment or wax paper between fragile or decorated cookies between layers can provide additional protection. Utilizing sturdy and appropriately sized boxes prevents cookies from shifting during shipping.

Cushioning the cookies within the packaging is equally important. Adding padding around the cookies, such as bubble wrap or crumpled parchment paper, helps absorb shocks and impacts during transit. The goal is to create a snug and secure environment within the packaging to minimize movement and reduce the risk of breakage. Careful placement of the cookies within the box and ensuring that there is no space can go a long way in preserving their pristine condition.

Temperature control is essential, especially when shipping chocolate- or frosting-covered cookies. Cookies may be susceptible to temperature variations resulting in melting or deterioration, depending on the destination and time of year. To mitigate this risk, consider shipping during cooler months or opting for expedited shipping services. Additionally, including ice packs or gel packs within the packaging, especially for shipments to warmer climates, can help maintain a more relaxed environment and protect against heat-related issues.

Choosing a suitable shipping carrier is a critical decision in the shipping process. Different carriers offer various services and shipping times, so selecting one that aligns with the desired delivery timeframe is essential. Additionally, inquire about shipping policies and whether the chosen carrier has specific guidelines for shipping perishable items like cookies. Some airlines may offer unique packaging options or advice on protecting delicate shipments.

In addition to being essential from a logistical standpoint, properly labeling the package helps ensure that the shipping is successful. Marking the box as "fragile" or "perishable" alerts shipping personnel to handle the package carefully. Including clear shipping labels with the recipient's name, address, and contact information ensures accurate delivery. For added precaution, consider adding a "this side up" label to indicate the proper orientation of the package.

Timing is another critical aspect of shipping cookies. Plan the shipping date to coincide with the desired arrival date, factoring in potential delays during peak shipping seasons or adverse weather conditions. Shipping earlier in the week is advisable to avoid packages sitting in transit over the weekend. Additionally, communicating with the recipient about the expected arrival date can help ensure someone is available to receive the package promptly.

Consider insurance for high-value or particularly delicate shipments. While carriers take measures to handle packages with care, accidents can happen during transit. Insuring the shipment provides financial protection in case of damage or loss, offering peace of mind to both the sender and the recipient. Understanding the carrier's insurance policies and procedures is essential in making informed decisions about investing in additional coverage.

Providing clear and concise instructions to the recipient can help ensure a smooth delivery experience. Please include information on handling the package upon arrival, whether refrigerating certain cookies or opening the box immediately. Providing storage recommendations, especially for cookies with perishable ingredients, helps the recipient enjoy the treats at their best.

Lastly, embracing technology can enhance the shipping process. To monitor the package's journey in real-time, utilize shipping carriers' online tracking services. This allows both the sender and the recipient to stay informed about the shipment's status and estimated delivery time. Additionally, consider sending the recipient a confirmation email or message with the tracking information, creating anticipation and allowing them to prepare for the package's arrival.

In conclusion, successfully shipping cookies requires a thoughtful approach encompassing cookie selection, meticulous packaging, temperature control, carrier selection, labeling, timing, insurance consideration, clear instructions, and tracking technology. By paying attention to these tips, amateur bakers and small businesses can ensure that their carefully crafted cookies reach their destination in pristine condition, ready to be enjoyed with the same delight as when they first emerged from the oven. Whether the goal is to spread holiday cheer, participate in a cookie exchange, or share a taste of homemade goodness, the art of shipping cookies becomes an integral part of the joyous tradition of giving and savoring delightful treats.

Creating cookie gift baskets

Creating cookie gift baskets is a delightful and personal way to share the joy of homemade treats with friends, family, or colleagues. These carefully curated baskets go beyond a simple batch of cookies; they become a thoughtful and visually appealing ensemble that elevates gifting to a festive and heartwarming experience. Crafting cookie gift baskets involves a blend of creativity, consideration, and culinary artistry, transforming a collection of cookies into a memorable and cherished present.

The foundation of an exquisite cookie gift basket lies in the selection of cookies. The variety and types of cookies contribute to the gift's overall appeal and enjoyment. Consider a mix of textures, flavors, and shapes to create a diverse and enticing assortment. Classic choices such as chocolate chip cookies, shortbread, and gingerbread provide a familiar base while incorporating unique and seasonal varieties that add a touch of excitement. The art lies in balancing well-loved classics and innovative flavors, ensuring each cookie contributes to the overall sensory experience.

Packaging plays a pivotal role in the visual allure of cookie gift baskets. The choice of baskets, boxes, or containers sets the tone for the presentation. Opt for baskets in festive colors or themes that align with the occasion or season. Woven baskets add a rustic touch, while elegant boxes or tins provide a more refined aesthetic. The goal is to create a visually appealing canvas that complements the cookies and enhances the overall gifting experience. Lining the basket with festive tissue paper or parchment paper adds an extra layer of charm, creating a cozy nest for the cookies.

Layering is an artful technique that adds depth and dimension to cookie gift baskets. Arrange the cookies in an organized and visually pleasing manner, considering aesthetics and practicality. For example, place more giant cookies at the back of the basket and smaller ones towards the front to ensure each type is visible. Interspersing cookies of different shapes and sizes create a dynamic and inviting display. To prevent breakage, consider using cupcake liners, mini cupcake wrappers, or parchment paper between layers, providing a protective barrier while maintaining the cookies' freshness.

Incorporating a theme into the cookie gift basket adds a delightful touch and enhances the overall cohesiveness of the presentation. The occasion and season can inspire the article or the recipient's preferences. For a holiday-themed basket, include cookies shaped like festive symbols such as stars, snowflakes, or Christmas trees. Alternatively, include spiced cookies infused with cinnamon, nutmeg, and cloves for a cozy winter theme. A themed approach adds a personal touch and showcases the effort and thought invested in creating a unique and tailored gift.

Adding decorative elements enhances the visual appeal of cookie gift baskets and transforms them into festive masterpieces. Consider incorporating holiday-themed ornaments, ribbons, or bows to complement the theme. Attach a personalized gift tag or card with a heartfelt message to convey warm wishes and add a personal touch. Tie twine or raffia around the basket for a rustic feel, creating a charming and homespun look. The decorative elements are the finishing touches that elevate the presentation from a simple assortment of cookies to a thoughtful and visually stunning gift.

Consider including a mix of cookies that cater to different tastes and preferences for a truly personalized touch. If the recipient has a sweet tooth, include indulgent and decadent cookies such as double chocolate fudge or caramel pecan delights. For those who enjoy a balance of sweet and savory, incorporate cookies with ingredients like nuts, seeds, or dried fruits. Consider dietary preferences, including gluten-free, vegan, or low-sugar options, for a thoughtful and inclusive gift. The key is creating a well-rounded assortment catering to the recipient's tastes and preferences.

To enhance the overall experience, consider including complementary treats or accompaniments in the cookie gift basket. This could be a specialty coffee or tea bag, a jar of homemade preserves, or an assortment of gourmet chocolates. The additional treats provide variety and elevate the gift to a more indulgent and luxurious experience. A carefully curated selection of accompanying items enhances the theme and creates a well-rounded and memorable gift basket.

Embracing seasonal flavors and ingredients adds a festive touch to cookie gift baskets. During the holidays, incorporate spices like cinnamon, ginger, and nutmeg, or include cookies adorned with holiday-themed decorations. In the spring, consider floral-infused cookies or those featuring vibrant colors. Seasonal fruits, such as berries or citrus, can be incorporated to add freshness and a seasonal twist. Adapting the flavors and themes to the time of year creates a dynamic and ever-changing array of cookie gift baskets that capture the essence of each season.

For those with a flair for baking, consider including a mix of homemade cookies and store-bought delights in the gift basket. Homemade cookies convey a sense of warmth and care, while carefully selected artisanal or specialty cookies add a layer of gourmet sophistication. This combination allows the gift giver to showcase their baking skills while introducing the recipient to unique, high-quality treats they may not have encountered. The mix of homemade and store-bought cookies creates a well-balanced and diverse assortment.

Consider providing information about the cookies in the gift basket to cater to the recipient's convenience. Attach a small note or label with the name of each cookie and a brief description of its flavors or ingredients. This adds a personal touch and allows the recipient to easily navigate the assortment, especially if they have dietary preferences or allergies. Including a simple guide enhances the overall experience and makes the gift more accessible and enjoyable.

In conclusion, creating cookie gift baskets is an art that blends culinary craftsmanship with thoughtful presentation. Each step makes a memorable and visually appealing gift, from selecting cookies and packaging choices to layering, thematic incorporation, and decorative elements. Giving a cookie gift basket transcends a simple exchange of treats; it becomes a heartfelt expression of care, creativity, and the joy of sharing delicious moments. Whether transferred during the holidays, as a birthday surprise, or to celebrate a special occasion, cookie gift baskets become tokens of warmth and delight, fostering a sense of connection and appreciation long after the last cookie is savored.

CHAPTER VIII

Cookie Decorating Techniques

Royal icing basics

Royal icing, a versatile and iconic baking decorating medium, can transform ordinary cookies into edible art. Royal icing has three essential ingredients: water, egg whites or meringue powder, and confectioners' sugar. It has a glossy, smooth surface that allows for many decorating options. Knowing the fundamentals of royal icing opens the door to a world of elaborate patterns, vivid colors, and polished-looking decorations. It's more than just a skill.

At its core, royal icing comprises confectioners' sugar, providing the sweetness and structure necessary for creating a smooth and firm surface on cookies. The sugar is combined with a liquid component, traditionally egg whites, to form a thick, pipeable consistency. However, recognizing raw egg consumption concerns, many bakers opt for meringue powder—an egg white substitute made from dried egg whites, sugar, and stabilizers. This alternative ensures both safety and convenience while maintaining the essential properties of traditional royal icing.

The key to achieving the right royal icing consistency lies in the ratio of sugar to liquid. The base consistency, often called "stiff" royal icing, is ideal for outlining and creating intricate details. Confectioners' sugar is gradually added to the liquid to get this rigidity, making the mixture lump-free and smooth. To generate a "flood" or "medium" consistency, more liquid (such as water or lemon juice) is added after the stiff feeling is reached. This step is essential for creating a smooth and even surface by filling in the highlighted regions.

Coloring royal icing opens the door to a spectrum of possibilities, and gel or paste food coloring is the preferred choice. The concentrated nature of these colorants ensures vibrant hues without compromising the consistency of the icing. Achieving a range of colors involves experimentation and understanding color theory. A small amount of dye is sufficient for pastel shades, while achieving deep or dark colors may require more. Start with a small amount and gradually add until the desired color is reached.

Working with royal icing begins with outlining the design using stiff consistency icing. This acts as a barrier, keeping the flood consistency icing inside the designated bounds. Once the outline has been set, the flood-consistency icing is gently poured or piped into the outlined area, allowing it to flow and evenly cover the surface. An offset spatula or toothpick can guide the icing into corners or edges to achieve a smooth finish. The magic of royal icing comes to life as the colors meld together, creating a seamless and polished surface.

The drying time of royal icing is a critical factor in the decorating process. The initial drying or setting time for outlined designs is essential before flooding with the medium consistency icing. It ensures that the flood icing remains within the outlines, preventing bleeding or blending of colors. While the surface may appear dry after a short period, allowing the cookies to dry completely— usually overnight—ensures a sturdy and durable finish.

Additional features and embellishments can be applied once the base layer dries. Edible decorations like sprinkles, edible pearls, or fondant shapes can be attached with royal icing. At this point, elaborate patterns, textures, and layers can be added to the cookies to give them depth and eye appeal. Many techniques, including brush embroidery, detailed piped lace patterns, marbling, and wet-on-wet designs, can be executed with royal icing due to its adaptability.

Beyond its decorative prowess, royal icing is a

preservation method for decorated cookies. The dry and firm finish acts as a protective layer, preventing the cookies from becoming stale and maintaining the integrity of the design. Once the royal icing has thoroughly dried, cookies can be stored in airtight containers, making them suitable for gifting or display over an extended period.

Troubleshooting is an inevitable aspect of working with

royal icing and understanding common issues can contribute to success in decorating. One frequent challenge is air bubbles within the icing, which can result in an uneven finish. To address this, gently tapping the flooded cookie on the countertop or using a toothpick to release trapped air can remedy the problem. Additionally, achieving the right consistency is crucial; if the icing is too thin, it may overflow the outlines, while overly stiff icing can be challenging to pipe or spread. Adjusting the liquid content gradually and testing the consistency ensures precision in decorating.

Humidity poses another challenge: it can impact the

drying time and finish of royal icing. The drying process may take longer in high-humidity environments, increasing the risk of color bleeding or blending. Using a fan or dehumidifier in decorating can help mitigate these challenges. Conversely, royal icing may dry too quickly in low-humidity conditions, leading to potential cracking or brittleness and covering cookies with a damp cloth. At the same time, drying can slow the drying process and promote a smooth finish.

While royal icing is a versatile and widely used decorating

medium, alternative options cater to specific preferences and dietary restrictions. Fondant, a pliable sugar paste, provides a smooth and matte finish and is often used for covering cakes and creating three-dimensional decorations. Buttercream, a rich and creamy frosting made with butter, confectioners' sugar, and flavorings, offers a softer and more indulgent alternative to royal icing. Each option has unique characteristics, allowing decorators to choose based on taste, texture, and the desired aesthetic.

In conclusion, royal icing is not merely a decorative element but a gateway to turning cookies into edible canvases. Its simplicity of ingredients belies the complexity of the designs and techniques it can facilitate. Mastering the basics of royal icing—understanding consistency, coloring, outlining, flooding, and drying— opens up a world of creative possibilities for bakers and decorators. Whether crafting cookies for special occasions or holidays or simply for the joy of edible art, royal icing stands as a testament to the sweet intersection of craftsmanship and creativity in baking.

Piping and flooding techniques

Piping and flooding techniques are the dynamic duos that elevate cookie decorating from a simple endeavor to a captivating art form. These fundamental techniques, primarily employed with royal icing, allow bakers and decorators to bring intricate designs, vibrant colors, and professional finishes to their creations. Mastering the art of piping and flooding involves understanding the nuances of consistency, precision, and layering, transforming cookies into edible canvases that captivate the eyes and delight the taste buds.

At the heart of cookie decorating with royal icing lies the technique of piping—the skillful art of outlining designs or creating intricate details on cookies. Piping consistency, often referred to as "stiff" royal icing, is the foundation for this technique. Achieving the right stiffness involves gradually incorporating confectioners' sugar into the liquid component, traditionally egg whites or meringue powder. The resulting mixture should be thick and smooth, holding its shape when piped through a decorating bag fitted with a fine tip.

The decorator can outline the desired design on the cookie once the piping consistency is reached. This step serves as a crucial boundary, defining the edges and preventing the flood consistency icing from spreading beyond the intended areas. The precision of the piping technique determines the final design's clarity and structure. Experienced decorators can use piping to create intricate patterns, delicate lacework, or bold outlines, showcasing the versatility and finesse achievable with royal icing.

After outlining, the flooding technique comes into play, transforming the outlined design into a smooth and seamless surface. Flood consistency icing, achieved by adding additional liquid to the stiff icing, has a thinner and more fluid consistency. This allows it to flow smoothly over the outlined areas, creating an even and level surface. The flooding technique is particularly effective for covering larger areas with a consistent layer of icing, resulting in a polished finish that serves as the canvas for further embellishments.

Timing is a critical factor when transitioning from piping to flooding. Allowing the outlined design to set or dry slightly ensures that the flood icing remains within the boundaries, preventing colors from bleeding into one another. The initial drying time creates a stable foundation for the flood icing to adhere to, contributing to the overall durability and longevity of the decorated cookies. While the outlined areas may appear dry after a short period, allowing the cookies to dry completely—typically overnight—ensures a flawless and resilient finish.

Coloring royal icing introduces an additional layer of creativity to piping and flooding techniques. Gel or paste food coloring is the preferred choice due to its concentrated nature, offering vibrant and true-to-color shades without compromising the consistency of the icing. Achieving a broad spectrum of colors involves understanding color theory and experimenting with different combinations. From pastel hues to deep and rich tones, decorators can customize their palette to suit the theme, occasion, or personal preference.

The process of piping and flooding involves a sequence of deliberate steps, each contributing to the overall success of the decorated cookies. The outlined design, meticulously piped onto the cookie, serves as a guide for the flood icing. The flood-consistency icing is gently poured or directed into the outlined area, allowing it to flow and cover the surface evenly. A gentle shake or tap on the countertop helps the flood icing settle and achieve a smooth finish. The magic unfolds as the colors blend seamlessly, creating a visually stunning and professionally executed design.

The layering aspect of flooding allows decorators to experiment with depth and dimension in their designs. By using flood consistency icing of different colors, decorators can create multi-dimensional effects, gradients, or visually interesting patterns. This layering technique adds complexity and visual interest to the decorated cookies, transforming them from simple treats into edible works of art. Whether creating ombre effects, intricate patterns, or vibrant landscapes, the flooding technique opens the door to endless possibilities.

Precision in piping and flooding extends beyond the actual techniques to the tools used in decorating. Decorating bags are crucial for accomplishing varied effects and intricacy, fitting with different tips. Fine tips are ideal for intricate outlines and delicate details, while more extensive tips facilitate the smooth flow of flood consistency icing for covering larger areas. Couplers allow decorators to switch directions without changing the bag, providing efficiency and convenience. Mastering these tools will enable decorators to express their creativity with precision and finesse.

As decorators advance in their skills, they often explore advanced piping techniques that add sophistication and flair to their designs. Wet-on-wet methods involve piping different colors onto the flooded surface while still wet, allowing them to blend seamlessly for marbled or tie-dye effects. Brush embroidery uses a damp brush to create textured patterns on the flooded surface, adding a hand- painted appearance. You may obtain the layered or dimensional look by letting one layer of flood icing dry completely before applying another. These sophisticated methods highlight royal icing's adaptability and capacity to produce elaborate and stunning designs.

The journey of mastering piping and flooding techniques is challenging. Air bubbles within the icing can result in an uneven finish, disrupting the smooth surface decorators aim to achieve. Gently tapping the flooded cookie on the countertop or using a toothpick to release trapped air addresses this issue. Achieving the right consistency is crucial; if the icing is too thin, it may overflow the outlines, while overly stiff icing can be challenging to pipe or spread. Gradually adjusting the liquid content and testing the consistency ensures precision in decorating. Humidity levels in the decorating environment also play a role in the success of piping and flooding techniques. The drying process may take longer in high-humidity conditions, and the risk of color bleeding or blending increases. Using a fan or dehumidifier in decorating can help mitigate these challenges. Conversely, royal icing may dry too quickly in low-humidity conditions, leading to potential cracking or brittleness and covering cookies with a damp cloth. At the same time, drying can slow the drying process and promote a smooth finish.

The beauty of piping and flooding techniques lies not only in their technical execution but also in their adaptability to various themes and occasions. From simple and elegant designs for weddings and anniversaries to playful and whimsical creations for birthdays or holidays, these techniques offer a versatile canvas for creative expression. The adaptability of royal icing allows decorators to bring to life a diverse array of designs, catering to different tastes, preferences, and celebrations.

In conclusion, piping and flooding techniques are the dynamic duo that empowers decorators to transform cookies into edible masterpieces. The precision of piping outlines and the seamless flow of flood consistency icing create a visually stunning canvas for creative expression. From mastering essential consistency and coloring to exploring advanced techniques and overcoming challenges, decorators embark on a journey of discovery and artistic exploration. Through the magic of piping and flooding, cookies transcend their humble origins, becoming sweet treats and edible works of art that captivate the eyes and delight the senses.

Edible glitter and embellishments

Edible glitter and embellishments add a touch of enchantment to the world of baking and cake decorating, transforming ordinary treats into dazzling confections that captivate the eyes and taste buds alike. These edible adornments, often made from sugar, gelatin, or starch ingredients, allow bakers and decorators to infuse a sense of magic and elegance into their creations. From shimmering dust to intricate shapes and designs, edible glitter and embellishments open a realm of possibilities, turning desserts into edible art.

At the forefront of edible decorations is the magical allure of edible glitter. Unlike traditional glitter, which is made from non-edible materials like plastic or metal, edible glitter is crafted from ingredients that are safe for consumption. Sugar or gum Arabic forms the base for many edible glitters, ensuring the sparkle they impart is visually stunning and entirely edible. Available in a dazzling array of colors and finishes, edible glitter adds a glamorous touch to cookies, cakes, cupcakes, and other sweet creations.

One of the popular forms of edible glitter is dust, which comes in fine, powder-like consistency. Edible glitter dust can be dusted directly onto the surface of desserts or mixed with clear alcohol or extract to create a paintable glaze for more intricate designs. The delicate shimmer it imparts elevates the visual appeal of desserts, making them ideal for special occasions like weddings, birthdays, or festive celebrations. Edible glitter dust comes in metallic and non-metallic finishes, allowing decorators to achieve a range of effects from subtle elegance to bold glamour.

For those seeking a more dimensional and eye-catching effect, edible glitter in the form of flakes or sequins provides a captivating solution. These larger particles of edible glitter create a textured and dynamic appearance on desserts, catching and reflecting light for a dazzling effect. Edible glitter flakes are particularly popular for decorating cupcakes, cookies, and desserts, where a sparkle can elevate the overall presentation. The versatility of edible glitter in various forms allows decorators to tailor their choices based on the desired aesthetic and the occasion's theme.

Beyond the enchanting world of glitter, edible embellishments encompass various decorative elements that bring creativity and personality to desserts. Fondant shapes, molded chocolates, and edible pearls are just a few examples of embellishments that add sophistication and flair to cakes and confections. Fondant, a pliable sugar paste, can be rolled out and shaped into intricate designs, creating three-dimensional decorations that range from flowers and bows to themed characters or motifs. Fondant provides a smooth and matte finish, making it an ideal medium for creating polished and refined decorations.

Molded chocolates, crafted using edible chocolate and specialized molds, allow decorators to add visual appeal and a rich chocolatey flavor to their creations. These chocolates can take on various shapes and forms, from delicate curls and swirls to themed designs that complement the overall theme of the dessert. Edible pearls, often made from sugar or fondant, provide a classic and elegant touch. Whether used individually or strung together in edible necklaces, pearls add a timeless and sophisticated element to cakes and cupcakes.

Edible gold or silver leaf is another delightful embellishment that has recently gained popularity. These ultra-thin sheets of precious metal add a touch of luxury and opulence to desserts, creating an elegant and indulgent visual spectacle. Edible gold or silver leaf can be delicately applied to the surface of cakes, cookies, or chocolates, imparting a lustrous finish that catches the light and draws attention to the intricate details of the dessert. Edible precious metal leaf is particularly prevalent in upscale events, weddings, and celebratory occasions.

Beyond the visual appeal, edible embellishments contribute to desserts' overall texture and flavor profile. Chocolate curls or shavings, for example, provide a visually striking element and introduce a rich and decadent chocolate flavor. Edible flowers, crafted from ingredients like gum paste or fondant, offer a delicate and botanical touch that enhances the sensory experience. Integrating these embellishments into desserts goes beyond aesthetics, creating a multi-sensory delight that elevates the enjoyment of the sweet treats.

For decorators seeking a whimsical and playful touch, edible glitters and embellishments come in various shapes and colors that cater to different themes and occasions. From edible stars and hearts to intricate lace patterns and geometric shapes, these embellishments allow decorators to bring their creative visions to life. Themed celebrations, such as birthdays, baby showers, or seasonal festivities, provide the perfect opportunity to explore the diversity of edible shapes and designs. Customizing desserts with these playful elements adds a personal and celebratory touch that resonates with the occasion and the preferences of those indulging in the treats.

Applying edible glitter and embellishments requires a thoughtful approach to balance and composition. While these elements can undoubtedly enhance the visual appeal of desserts, an overabundance can overwhelm the overall design. A harmonious balance involves considering the dessert's theme, color palette, and overall aesthetic. Careful placement of edible glitter and embellishments ensures that they complement rather than compete with the other design elements, allowing each decoration to shine and contribute to the cohesive beauty of the dessert.

Adhering edible glitter and embellishments to desserts involves various techniques, depending on the decoration's nature and surface. For flat surfaces like cookies or cakes, a light misting of water or a thin layer of clear piping gel can be an adhesive for edible glitter or fondant shapes; for three-dimensional elements like fondant flowers or chocolate decorations, a small amount of royal icing or melted chocolate acts as a secure and edible glue. The choice of adhesive depends on the specific requirements of the decoration and the type of dessert being adorned.

The realm of edible glitter and embellishments extends beyond cakes and cookies to include cupcakes, chocolates, and beverages. Cupcakes, adorned with edible glitter or topped with fondant shapes, become miniature works of art that are as delightful to look at as they are to eat. Chocolates, molded into intricate shapes and dusted with edible glitter, offer chocolate enthusiasts a luxurious and indulgent treat. Even beverages can be adorned with edible glitter, turning drinks into shimmering concoctions that add a touch of magic to celebrations and events.

As with any decorative element, considerations for dietary preferences and restrictions play a role in the choice of edible glitter and embellishments. Fortunately, the market offers a variety of options, including vegan, gluten-free, and allergen-free alternatives, ensuring that everyone can enjoy the visual spectacle of adorned desserts. Reading product labels and verifying the ingredients with manufacturers helps decorators make informed choices that align with the dietary needs of their audience.

In conclusion, edible glitter and embellishments bring a touch of magic and artistry to baking and cake decorating. From shimmering dust to three-dimensional fondant shapes, these edible adornments allow decorators to infuse their creations with elegance, whimsy, and visual intrigue. The versatility of edible glitter and embellishments caters to various themes and occasions, making them a staple for celebrations, weddings, birthdays, and festive events. Beyond their visual appeal, these edible elements contribute to desserts' overall texture and flavor, creating a multi-sensory experience that elevates the joy of indulging in sweet treats. Whether used sparingly for a touch of sophistication or lavishly for a dazzling display, edible glitter, and embellishments stand as a testament to

CHAPTER IX

Hosting a Cookie Swap

Planning and organizing a cookie swap

Planning and organizing a cookie swap is a delightful way to celebrate the holiday season or any special occasion, bringing together friends, family, or colleagues in a spirit of warmth, sharing, and delicious treats. A cookie swap is a festive gathering where participants bake and exchange batches of homemade cookies, creating a diverse assortment that adds joy to the festivities. The success of a cookie swap lies not only in the delicious cookies but also in the thoughtful planning and organization that goes into creating a memorable and enjoyable event.

The first step in planning a cookie swap is establishing the event's logistics. Considering the participants ' convenience, decide on the date, time, and location. With its inherent sense of merriment, the holiday season is an ideal time for a cookie swap, but any time of the year can be suitable for this heartwarming gathering. Ensure that the chosen location is spacious enough to accommodate all participants comfortably, with ample room for displaying and exchanging cookies. Whether held in a cozy living room, a communal space, or even virtually, the setting should encourage a sense of camaraderie and festive cheer.

Once the logistical details are in place, the next crucial aspect is determining the number of participants and establishing ground rules for the cookie swap. Communicate the guidelines clearly to ensure a harmonious and enjoyable exchange. Decide on the minimum and maximum number of cookies each participant should bring, allowing for variety without overwhelming anyone. Setting guidelines for the type of cookies—whether they should be holiday-themed, allergy-friendly, or of a specific flavor—adds a thematic element and ensures a well-curated assortment. Transparency and open communication contribute to a shared understanding, fostering a positive and inclusive atmosphere.

Invitations are pivotal in creating excitement and anticipation for the cookie swap. Craft invitations that reflect the festive spirit of the event, incorporating themes, colors, or images associated with cookies and holiday cheer. Clearly outline the date, time, location, and specific guidelines for the cookie swap. If the event is virtual, provide details on how participants can drop off or exchange cookies. Encourage creativity and personalization in the invitations, setting the tone for the upcoming occasion. Use digital platforms like email or social media for efficient communication and coordination.

To ensure a diverse array of cookies at the swap, consider coordinating the types of cookies participants plan to bake. To do this, you can use a sign-up form or have a simple conversation where people proclaim they will bake. This coordination guarantees that a range of flavors and textures are included in the finished selection and helps prevent repetition. Encourage participants to try various recipes, from time-honored favorites to creative and original concoctions, to give a surprise aspect to the cookie exchange.

Consider incorporating a theme into the cookie swap to enhance the festive atmosphere further. Whether it's a holiday theme, a specific flavor profile, or a creative twist, a piece adds a cohesive and decorative element to the event. Participants can align their cookie choices with the music, creating a visually appealing and thematic display. Themes also inspire decorations, table settings, and even festive attire, adding a layer of fun and celebration to the cookie swap.

Organizing a cookie swap involves coordinating the logistics of the cookie exchange. Each participant should bring enough cookies for each person to take a shared home, and an efficient system for distributing the cookies is essential. One popular method is the round-robin approach, where participants move randomly, exchanging cookies with each person. An alternative would be to put up a central display area where participants could peruse and choose cookies. Contactless drop-off, scheduled pickup dates, and mailing options are available for virtual cookie swaps, allowing participants to share their adorable creations.

Encourage participants to share the stories or traditions behind their chosen cookie recipes. This adds a personal and meaningful touch to the event, fostering a sense of connection and community. Consider providing recipe cards or a digital compilation of the recipes to participants, allowing them to recreate the delicious treats at home. The exchange of recipes becomes a cherished takeaway, creating a lasting connection between participants beyond the cookie swap itself.

As a host, consider adding additional festive touches to the cookie swap. Decorate the space with holiday-themed décor, such as garlands, twinkling lights, or themed centerpieces. Arrange the cookies on festive platters or trays, creating an inviting and visually appealing display. Consider providing hot beverages, such as cocoa or spiced cider, to complement the sweet treats and add to the overall warmth of the gathering. The attention to these details contributes to the overall ambiance and ensures that the cookie swap is not just a culinary exchange but a memorable and enjoyable experience.

Consider implementing a cookie labeling system to accommodate participants with dietary restrictions or preferences. Participants can indicate if their cookies are gluten-free, nut-free, vegan, or any other relevant information. This thoughtful approach allows everyone to enjoy the treats without concerns about allergies or dietary restrictions. Clear labeling also contributes to an inclusive atmosphere, where participants can navigate the assortment with ease and confidence.

Photography adds an extra layer of enjoyment to the cookie swap. Encourage participants to capture the beauty of their cookies before the exchange begins. Whether through individual photos or group shots, documenting the array of cookies creates lasting memories and provides participants with a visual record of the delightful assortment. Share pictures on social media platforms or create a digital album to extend the joy of the cookie swap beyond the event itself.

After the cookie swap concludes, express gratitude to participants for their contributions and for making the event successful. Consider sending thank-you notes or messages to convey appreciation for their time, effort, and delicious cookies. A small token of appreciation, such as a festive cookie cutter or a jar of homemade jam, adds a thoughtful touch and serves as a memento of the special occasion. Acknowledging participants' efforts fosters a sense of community and ensures the cookie swap becomes a cherished tradition.

In conclusion, planning and organizing a cookie swap is a heartwarming and festive undertaking that brings people together to share the joy of homemade treats. From establishing logistics and ground rules to coordinating cookie types and incorporating themes, thoughtful planning sets the stage for a successful and enjoyable event. Invitations, decorations, and additional festive touches contribute to the overall ambiance, creating a delightful atmosphere for the cookie exchange. With attention to detail and camaraderie, a cookie swap becomes more than just a culinary event—it becomes a cherished tradition that brings people together in the heart of warmth, sharing, and the sweetness of homemade cookies.

Recipes for a successful event

Recipes for a successful event go beyond the culinary delights served; they encompass a careful blend of thoughtful planning, engaging execution, and an atmosphere that resonates with the spirit of the occasion. As a chef meticulously selects ingredients to create a harmonious dish, event planners curate elements to contribute to a memorable and enjoyable experience. The success of an event lies in the artful combination of critical components, each playing a unique role in crafting a delightful and seamless gathering.

The first essential ingredient for a successful event is meticulous planning. Whether it's a neighborhood event, a corporate get-together, or a celebratory occasion, this requires identifying the goals and purposes of the gathering. Clearly outlining goals and expectations lays the foundation for subsequent decisions and actions. Establishing a realistic budget is another crucial step, ensuring that resources are allocated efficiently, and priorities are aligned with the overall vision. A well-thought-out timeline serves as a roadmap, guiding the planning process from initial preparations to the day of the event. Meticulous planning sets the stage for a well-organized and stress-free execution.

Engaging invitations serve as a flavorful introduction to any event. Just as a chef strives to entice diners with a delicious menu, event planners aim to captivate attendees from the moment they receive the invitation. Thoughtful design, precise details, and a touch of creativity contribute to invitations that convey essential information and set the tone for the gathering. Whether delivered digitally or in print, invitations preview the event's atmosphere and provide a glimpse into the experience awaiting attendees.

The venue serves as the backdrop for the event, shaping its ambiance, contributing to the overall experience, and choosing a platform that aligns with the event's theme, size, and objectives. A well-selected venue provides the canvas on which the event unfolds, whether it's an elegant ballroom for a formal affair, a cozy setting for an intimate gathering, or an outdoor space for a casual celebration. Considerations such as accessibility, amenities, and the overall atmosphere play a role in creating the desired environment for attendees.

Culinary offerings are the centerpiece of many events, and the menu is pivotal in leaving a lasting impression. Whether it's a formal dinner, a buffet, or a selection of hors d'oeuvres, the menu should cater to the preferences and dietary needs of the attendees. A well-balanced and diverse menu adds to the overall enjoyment of the event. Collaborating with skilled caterers or chefs ensures that the culinary experience aligns with the theme and tone of the gathering. The presentation of the food, attention to detail, and the inclusion of signature dishes contribute to a memorable dining experience.

Entertainment injects vitality into an event, creating joy, engagement, and connection moments. The choice of entertainment should complement the event's theme and resonate with the audience's preferences. Live music, performances, or interactive activities add a dynamic element, elevating the overall energy of the gathering. The goal is to create an immersive experience that captivates attendees and leaves a positive impression. Well-planned entertainment contributes to the atmosphere and helps forge lasting memories.

The décor of the event venue serves as the visual expression of its theme and sets the mood for the occasion. From floral arrangements and table settings to lighting and overall aesthetics, thoughtful décor enhances the atmosphere and creates a cohesive visual experience. The color palette, choice of materials, and attention to detail contribute to the overall ambiance. Whether aiming for elegance, warmth, or a festive atmosphere, the décor serves as a visual storyteller, conveying the essence of the event to attendees.

Seamless execution is the culmination of meticulous planning and attention to detail. The coordination of logistics, the timing of activities, and the responsiveness to unforeseen circumstances are critical aspects of a successful event. Well-trained and efficient event staff, including planners, caterers, and on-site coordinators, ensure the event unfolds smoothly. Effective communication among team members and quick problem-solving contribute to a stress-free experience for organizers and attendees.

Guest engagement and interaction are vital ingredients for a successful event. Creating opportunities for attendees to connect, share experiences, and participate in activities enhances enjoyment. Interactive elements, such as photo booths, networking sessions, or themed activities, encourage engagement and contribute to a lively atmosphere. Thoughtful consideration of the event flow ensures that attendees feel included and have opportunities to make meaningful connections.

A gracious and appreciative host adds a personal touch to the event, fostering a welcoming and inclusive atmosphere. The host sets the tone for the gathering, extending warmth and hospitality to attendees. A well-prepared and confident host ensures that the event progresses smoothly, addressing the audience, introducing speakers or performers, and expressing gratitude to participants. The host's ability to connect with the audience contributes to the sense of community and shared experience.

Post-event follow-up and feedback are the final components of a successful event. Gathering feedback from attendees provides valuable insights into what worked well and areas for improvement. Expressing gratitude to participants, sponsors, and contributors reinforces the sense of appreciation and leaves a positive impression. Following up with attendees through emails, surveys, or social media extends the connection beyond the event, fostering a sense of community and laying the groundwork for future engagements.

In conclusion, recipes for successful events are multi-faceted, incorporating meticulous planning, engaging invitations, carefully chosen venues, delectable culinary offerings, entertaining elements, thoughtfully designed décor, seamless execution, guest engagement, a gracious host, and post-event follow-up. Each piece uniquely contributes to crafting an event that meets its objectives and leaves a lasting and positive impression on attendees. Just as a well-executed dish brings together a symphony of flavors, a successful event harmonizes various elements to create an experience that delights the senses and lingers in the memories of those who attended.

Tips for a memorable gathering

Creating a memorable gathering is an art that goes beyond the mere logistics of planning and executing an event. It involves a thoughtful orchestration of elements designed to foster connection, joy, and lasting memories. Whether hosting a family celebration, a social gathering with friends, or a corporate event, the tips for creating a memorable group span a range of considerations, from the overall atmosphere to the finer details that contribute to the comfort and enjoyment of attendees.

The foundation for a successful gathering lies in setting clear intentions. Before delving into the planning details, articulate the community's purpose and objectives. Whether it's a milestone celebration, a networking event, or a casual get-together, a well-defined intention provides a guiding framework for subsequent decisions. It influences the venue choice, the event's tone, and the overall atmosphere, ensuring that every aspect aligns with the central theme.

The venue serves as the canvas for the gathering, shaping its ambiance and contributing significantly to the overall experience. Selecting the right venue involves considering the size of the guest list, the formality of the occasion, and the desired atmosphere. Whether it's an intimate dinner at home, a picturesque outdoor setting, or a sophisticated event space, the venue should complement the gathering's purpose and enhance the overall experience for attendees.

The ambiance of a gathering plays a crucial role in

shaping the mood and overall experience. Thoughtful attention to lighting, decorations, and background music can transform a space into a welcoming environment. Consider the sensory elements that contribute to a warm atmosphere—the soft glow of candles, the scent of fresh flowers, or the gentle background melodies. A welcoming atmosphere sets the stage for meaningful connections and positive interactions.

Infusing personal touches into the gathering creates a

sense of intimacy and consideration for attendees. Whether personalized decorations, custom details, or tailored elements reflect the event's theme, these touches demonstrate thoughtfulness and care. Personalization can extend to small gestures like name tags, welcome notes, or customized favors, making attendees feel acknowledged and valued.

The menu is a centerpiece of any gathering, and the

culinary offerings can significantly impact the overall experience. Consider the preferences and dietary restrictions of attendees when planning the menu. Whether it's a formal dinner, a buffet, or a selection of appetizers, the food should align with the theme and enhance the enjoyment of the gathering. Well-presented and high-quality culinary offerings leave a lasting impression on attendees.

Thoughtfully planned activities contribute to the vibrancy

of a gathering, providing opportunities for connection and

enjoyment. Tailor activities to the preferences and interests of attendees. Engaging activities, whether interactive workshops, games, or entertainment, add a dynamic element to the group. They encourage mingling, foster a sense of community, and contribute to creating memorable moments.

Striking a balance between structured activities and unstructured time allows attendees to enjoy the gathering at their own pace. While planned activities provide a framework for engagement, allowing for unstructured time enables organic connections and spontaneous conversations. A mix of both ensures that the gathering accommodates different preferences and comfort levels, contributing to a well-rounded and enjoyable experience.

Clear and timely communication is fundamental to the success of any gathering. Ensure attendees have all the necessary information, including the date, time, location, and specific instructions or guidelines. Utilize digital platforms for efficient communication, whether sending invitations, providing updates, or sharing relevant information. Open and transparent communication fosters a sense of anticipation and ensures that attendees are well-informed and prepared for the gathering.

Thoughtful details and surprises add an element of delight to the gathering. Consider incorporating unexpected elements, such as a themed photo booth, a surprise performance, or personalized touches that reflect the event's uniqueness. These thoughtful details contribute to the overall enjoyment and create moments that stand out in the attendees' memories. Surprise adds a layer of excitement and contributes to the gathering's memorability.

Every gathering goes differently than planned, and flexibility and adaptability are essential for success. Recognize that unexpected circumstances may arise, and be prepared to adjust plans as needed. A flexible approach allows hosts to navigate challenges gracefully and ensures that the gathering remains a positive and enjoyable experience for attendees. The ability to adapt to unforeseen circumstances contributes to the overall success of the event.

Expressing gratitude and acknowledging attendees is a meaningful way to end the gathering on a positive note. Take the time to thank guests for their presence and participation verbally during the event or through follow-up communication. Consider sending thank-you notes or small tokens of appreciation as a gesture of gratitude. Expressing appreciation creates a sense of connection and leaves attendees with a positive and memorable experience.

In conclusion, creating a memorable gathering is an intricate process that involves weaving together various elements with care and consideration. From the overarching intentions to the finer details, each aspect plays a crucial role in shaping an experience that resonates with attendees. A successful gathering is not merely an event; it is an opportunity to create moments that linger in the memories of those in attendance and contribute to a sense of community and shared celebration.

CHAPTER X

Holiday Cookie Traditions Around the World

Exploring global holiday cookie customs

The holiday season brings a tapestry of traditions and customs that vary globally, each thread woven with the unique flavors and textures of festive delights. Among these culinary traditions, holiday cookies stand out as sweet ambassadors of culture, carrying the essence of joyous celebrations and the warmth of shared moments. From the spiced aromas of gingerbread to the delicate crunch of sugar cookies, the world's holiday cookie customs reflect a rich tapestry of ingredients, techniques, and stories that transcend borders and unite us in the joy of the season.

The iconic Lebkuchen takes center stage in Germany, the land of enchanting Christmas markets and centuries-old traditions. These gingerbread cookies, rich with honey, spices, and almonds, have been a holiday staple since the 13th century. Often intricately decorated with icing, Lebkuchen cookies are not just a treat for the taste buds but also a feast for the eyes. The German holiday season is incomplete without these festive delights' sweet and aromatic presence, enjoyed with a mug of mulled wine against twinkling lights.

Venturing to Italy, we encounter the delicate and intricately patterned Pizzelle. These thin, crisp, waffle-like cookies are a beloved part of Italian holiday traditions. With their intricate designs, Pizzelle irons imprint the batter with festive patterns that vary by region. These cookies, which are vanilla- or anise-scented and inspire a sense of community, are frequently eaten with a cup of vino or espresso during the Christmas season. Each bite of Pizzelle is a tribute to Italian artistry, as the dish's simplicity conceals the expertise involved.

Crossing the Atlantic to Mexico, the holiday season welcomes the preparation of Bunuelos. These deep-fried, crispy dough rounds are often coated in cinnamon sugar, offering a delightful crunch with every bite. While Bunuelos are enjoyed year-round, they hold a special place in Mexican holiday celebrations. Families create these circular delights, forming a communal activity that amplifies the festive spirit. The warmth of the season is mirrored in the golden hues of Bunuelos, a testament to the joy of shared traditions.

In Sweden, the aromatic scent of pepparkakor wafts through homes during the holiday season. Pepparkakor, a traditional Swedish ginger snap, is spiced with cinnamon, ginger, and cloves. These thin, crisp cookies are often cut into intricate shapes and enjoyed as-is or used to construct edible gingerbread houses. The Swedish tradition of making and decorating Pepparkakor extends beyond households, with schools, communities, and workplaces often joining in the festivities, turning baking into a shared celebration of the season.

Journeying to the heart of France, we encounter the delicate Sablés. These buttery shortbread cookies, named for their sandy texture ("sable" means sand in French), are often shaped into simple rounds or more intricate designs. The French take pride in baking, and Sablés, with their rich buttery flavor and crumbly texture, embodies the elegance and finesse of French culinary traditions. Enjoyed with a cup of tea or coffee, Sablés capture the refined essence of French holiday celebrations.

Moving eastward to the Middle East, we find Ma'amoul, a beloved treat during festive occasions such as Eid. These filled cookies, made with semolina and butter, encase a sweet filling of dates, nuts, or figs. The intricate designs on the surface of Ma'amoul are often imprinted using wooden molds, showcasing the region's craftsmanship. Making Ma'amoul is a cherished family activity, with generations coming together to shape and fill these delightful cookies, reinforcing the bonds of kinship during festive times.

The classic Sugar Cookie takes on various forms and decorations in the United States during the holiday season. Whether adorned with colored icing, festive sprinkles, or shaped into holiday-themed figures, Sugar Cookies have become a canvas for creativity and personal expression. Decorating sugar cookies has become a cherished tradition in many American households, bringing families together for an afternoon of artistic exploration and delicious indulgence.

These glimpses into global holiday cookie customs reveal the universal nature of celebrating through food. Each cookie tells a story—a narrative of cultural heritage, familial bonds, and the joy of coming together to create something unique. In exploring these customs, we discover the common thread that unites us all during the holiday season—the desire to savor the richness of tradition, the sweetness of togetherness, and the joy found in the simple pleasure of sharing a delightful cookie with loved ones.

Learning about unique regional recipes

The vast diversity of civilizations and geographical areas is reflected in the fabric of world food, which is sewn together with a wide range of flavors, methods, and customs. Each corner of the globe boasts a unique culinary identity shaped by geography, climate, and the cultural tapestry of its people. Exploring and learning about regional recipes is like embarking on a gastronomic journey, unraveling the stories embedded in local ingredients, time-honored methods, and the communal spirit of sharing food.

In the heart of India, the vibrant and diverse culinary landscape is a testament to the country's cultural richness. One cannot delve into regional Indian recipes without encountering the fragrant and complex layers of Biriyani—a dish that encapsulates the artistry of Indian cooking. Hailing from Hyderabad, Hyderabadi Biriyani is a culinary masterpiece where fragrant basmati rice, succulent meat (often chicken or mutton), and a medley of aromatic spices are layered and slow-cooked to perfection. The result is a harmonious blend of flavors, each grain of rice infused with the essence of saffron, cardamom, and cloves. Biriyani is not just a dish; it is a celebration of culinary finesse, a reflection of the region's historical influences, and a culinary heritage passed down through generations.

In the sun-soaked hills of Tuscany, Italy, the simplicity and authenticity of Ribollita embody the essence of regional cooking. This hearty soup, born from the Tuscan peasant tradition, features vegetables, beans, and day-old bread. The magic of Ribollita lies in its humble origins and the resourcefulness of using readily available ingredients. The soup is a flavorful concoction that marries the earthiness of cannellini beans with the freshness of seasonal vegetables. Often prepared in large quantities and left to simmer, Ribollita is a dish that improves with time, capturing the essence of slow-cooked comfort in a bowl.

Crossing the Atlantic to the southern United States, we encounter the soulful flavors of Louisiana embodied in Gumbo. This regional stew, with roots in West African, French, and Spanish culinary traditions, celebrates the multicultural influences shaping the region. Gumbo is a rich and flavorful dish, typically featuring a dark roux, the "holy trinity" of vegetables (bell peppers, onions, and celery), and a medley of proteins such as chicken, sausage, and shellfish. The dish reflects Louisiana's cultural melting pot, showcasing the region's love for bold spices, aromatic herbs, and the communal act of sharing a pot of simmering goodness.

In the mountainous regions of Japan, the delicate art of Hōtō noodle soup reflects the culinary traditions of the Yamanashi Prefecture. This regional dish, originating in rustic mountain villages, features wide wheat noodles simmered in a miso-based broth with various vegetables. The simplicity of Hōtō is deceptive, as each bowl represents a harmonious balance of flavors and textures. The dish exemplifies the Japanese appreciation for seasonality, utilizing local produce and embracing the nourishing qualities of a warming bowl of soup amid the cool mountain air.

Traveling to the Middle East, the Levantine region introduces us to the culinary poetry of Muhammara—a pepper and walnut spread that hails from Syria. Muhammara is a symphony of sweet, smoky, and tangy notes, bursting with red peppers, walnuts, olive oil, and pomegranate molasses flavors. Beyond its culinary appeal, Muhammara serves as a cultural emblem, embodying the warmth of Middle Eastern hospitality and the tradition of breaking bread together. The dish exemplifies the region's emphasis on fresh, vibrant ingredients and the communal act of sharing a meal.

In the heartland of Mexico, the ancient technique of nixtamalization transforms humble corn into the foundation of traditional dishes like Tamales. These savory pockets of masa, filled with meats, beans, or chilies, are wrapped in corn husks and steamed to perfection. Tamales are more than a convenient way to enjoy a meal; they are a culinary canvas, reflecting Mexico's diverse regional variations and creative interpretations. From the spicy richness of Oaxacan Tamales to the tropical flavors of Veracruz, each region imparts its unique identity to this ancient Mesoamerican dish.

Back in the Mediterranean, the island of Cyprus presents a culinary gem in the form of Halloumi, a semi-hard cheese with a distinct texture that can withstand grilling and frying. This regional cheese, traditionally made from a blend of sheep and goat milk, has become a global sensation. Its unique ability to hold its shape under heat makes it a versatile ingredient in savory and sweet dishes. Halloumi represents the island's agricultural bounty and showcases the ingenuity of Cypriot farmers who turned a simple cheese into a culinary phenomenon.

Exploring these unique regional recipes unveils a world of culinary diversity, where each dish tells a story of cultural heritage, geographical influences, and the resourcefulness of communities. Whether it's the intricate layers of Hyderabadi Biriyani, the comforting warmth of Tuscan Ribollita, the soulful notes of Louisiana Gumbo, the delicate simplicity of Japanese Hōtō, the vibrant flavors of Levantine Muhammara, the ancient traditions of Mexican Tamales, or the versatile charm of Cypriot Halloumi, each recipe encapsulates the essence of its region. These dishes are not merely sustenance; they celebrate identity, a connection to the land, and an invitation.

Incorporating diverse flavors into your holiday baking

The holiday season is a time of festivity, warmth, and the aromatic embrace of freshly baked treats. As bakers embark on their seasonal culinary journeys, the opportunity arises to explore a kaleidoscope of flavors that extends beyond the traditional. While classic holiday spices like cinnamon, nutmeg, and ginger are cherished, embracing diverse flavors can elevate your baking to new heights, infusing your creations with a symphony of tastes that reflect the richness of global culinary traditions.

Diving into the world of diverse flavors, one might be inspired by the compelling notes of cardamom—a spice synonymous with warmth and depth. Cardamom, from the Indian subcontinent, gives baked goods a subtle flavor profile that dances on the palate by adding a zesty, floral fragrance. Whether incorporated into a spiced cake, gingerbread cookies, or even a luscious holiday bread, cardamom introduces an exotic twist that transports the palate to far-off lands, evoking the spirit of celebration in various cultural festivities.

Going a little deeper, the lovely, flowery perfume of lavender becomes apparent and is a delightful, unexpected addition to holiday cooking. Originating in the Mediterranean, lavender adds a delicate yet elegant flavor to shortbread biscuits, scones, or even a light cake. The fragrance of lavender can evoke memories of sun-drenched fields and leisurely afternoons, offering a unique sensory experience that transcends traditional holiday aromas.

From the heart of the Middle East comes the fragrant allure of rose water, a captivating essence that can transform your holiday treats into aromatic delights. In Lebanese and Persian cuisines, rose water is a common ingredient in pastries and sweets, imparting a delicate floral note that harmonizes with various baked goods. Whether used in sugar cookies, cupcakes, or even a festive trifle, rose water introduces a touch of elegance and a sensory journey reminiscent of blooming gardens and ancient traditions.

Including exotic fruits can also breathe life into your holiday baking repertoire. Consider the tropical brightness of passion fruit, which introduces a tangy sweetness when incorporated into glazes, fillings, or even a decadent cheesecake. Originating from South America, passion fruit brings a sunny disposition to the holiday table, infusing your treats with a vibrant twist contrasting the winter chill.

Traveling to the Far East, the nutty, buttery flavor of black sesame seeds emerges as a unique addition to holiday baking. Commonly used in Asian desserts, black sesame seeds lend a rich, toasty undertone that complements sweet and savory creations. From incorporating them into cookies or bars to experimenting with black sesame-infused doughs, this ingredient introduces a delightful complexity that invites a sense of culinary adventure to your holiday kitchen.

For those seeking a touch of nostalgia and comforting familiarity, exploring the depths of molasses can provide a rich, robust foundation for holiday treats. A staple in classic recipes like gingerbread cookies and molasses spice cake, this dark, syrupy sweetener brings a deep, caramelized flavor that resonates with the coziness of winter. From sugarcane processing, molasses connects bakers to centuries-old traditions, making it a timeless addition to holiday confections.

Incorporating diverse flavors into your holiday baking is not merely a culinary experiment but a celebration of cultural diversity and a way to bridge the gap between traditions. From the warm embrace of cardamom to the floral sophistication of lavender, the exotic allure of rose water, the tropical brightness of passion fruit, the nutty richness of black sesame, and the comforting depths of molasses, each flavor tells a story. These stories, woven into the fabric of your holiday treats, create a sensory experience that transcends borders, inviting those who indulge to embark on a journey of taste and tradition.

As you embark on your holiday baking adventure, consider the stories behind these diverse flavors. Allow the warmth of cardamom to transport you to Indian festivities, let the fragrance of lavender evoke Mediterranean landscapes, and embrace the exotic allure of rose water reminiscent of Middle Eastern celebrations. The tangy brightness of passion fruit can bring the tropics to your kitchen, black sesame seeds can add an Asian-inspired twist, and the comforting richness of molasses can connect you to time-honored recipes passed down through generations.

In conclusion, incorporating diverse flavors into your holiday baking allows you to expand your culinary horizons, celebrate global traditions, and infuse your creations with a touch of the unexpected. By embracing a spectrum of tastes that transcend the familiar, you elevate your baking to new heights and invite a sense of unity and cultural richness to your holiday table. So, as you gather your ingredients and embark on this festive culinary journey, let the diverse flavors of the world inspire you to create a tapestry of treats that reflect the global mosaic of holiday celebrations.

CHAPTER XI

Preserving Winter Magic

Storing Cookies for Freshness

In baking, creating delectable cookies marks a time-honored tradition that brings joy and satisfaction to bakers and those fortunate enough to indulge in these sweet treats. Yet, the pursuit of cookie perfection doesn't end with the final turn of the oven dial; equally important is the art of storing cookies for freshness. This crucial step ensures that the hard work and culinary creativity invested in crafting these delectable morsels are preserved, allowing cookies to maintain their texture, flavor, and overall quality over time.

Understanding the factors contributing to cookie staleness is paramount in devising effective storage strategies. With varying ingredients and textures, cookies are particularly susceptible to environmental influences. Exposure to air, moisture, and temperature fluctuations can swiftly compromise the freshness of even the most meticulously baked batches. Thus, storing cookies begins with recognizing these vulnerabilities and implementing measures to counteract their effects.

A fundamental consideration in storing cookies is the choice of container. Airtight containers, ranging from classic cookie tins to plastic or glass containers with secure lids, act as formidable barriers against air infiltration. By preventing exposure to oxygen, a leading culprit in staleness, these containers create a protective cocoon around the cookies, preserving their moisture content and original texture. Additionally, selecting containers with multiple compartments allows for the segregation of different cookie varieties, preventing the mingling of flavors and aromas that could compromise the distinct identity of each treat.

The strategic use of moisture-retaining elements is equally crucial in the battle against staleness. Adding a slice of bread or a small piece of apple to the cookie container might seem like a quaint tradition, but it serves a practical purpose. These moisture-rich companions act as natural humectants, absorbing excess dryness and maintaining the cookies' chewiness. But, to keep the bread and apples from growing mold, replacing them regularly is essential.

Temperature control emerges as another critical factor in the storage equation. Cookies are sensitive to extremes, whether excessive heat or chilly temperatures. Storing cookies in a cool, dry place, away from direct sunlight, helps to preserve their quality. Refrigeration is an option for certain cookie types, particularly those with perishable ingredients like cream or custard fillings. Care must ensure the cookies are well-wrapped to prevent the refrigerator scent from ruining their flavors.

In the context of longevity, the freezer emerges as a powerful ally in storing cookies for extended periods. Cookie batter or finished baked goods can be frozen to build a reserve of cookies that can be used whenever needed. When freezing cookie dough, it is advisable to shape it into individual portions before freezing. This facilitates convenient baking and minimizes the need to thaw an entire batch when a sudden cookie craving strikes. Fully baked cookies can also be frozen, provided they are adequately wrapped to guard against freezer burn.

However, the freezing process is not a one-size-fits-all solution. Different types of cookies may require varied approaches. For example, drop cookies, such as chocolate chip or oatmeal cookies, can be frozen in a single layer on a baking sheet before transferring to a container. On the other hand, delicate or intricate cookies, such as intricately decorated sugar cookies, may benefit from being individually wrapped before freezing to preserve their visual appeal.

While the physical aspects of storage play a pivotal role, timing is also a key consideration. Freshly baked cookies, though tempting to devour immediately, benefit from a brief settling period before being transferred to long-term storage. Allowing cookies to cool completely on a wire rack ensures that they reach an optimal texture and prevents the build-up of condensation within the storage container, which could contribute to sogginess.

Moreover, the type of cookie itself influences the optimal duration for storage. Certain cookies, particularly those with higher fat or moisture content, possess a shorter shelf life and are best enjoyed within a few days of baking. Conversely, cookies with lower moisture content, such as biscotti or shortbread, exhibit a longer staying power and can maintain their freshness for several weeks when stored appropriately.

In the quest for cookie freshness, one must recognize the role of thoughtful packaging. While airtight containers form the primary defense against staleness, additional layers of protection can be provided through careful wrapping. Individually wrapping cookies in parchment paper or wax paper before placing them in the container adds an extra barrier against air and moisture, ensuring that each cookie remains a miniature masterpiece, free from the clutches of staleness.

The considerations for storing cookies extend beyond the physical realm into flavor preservation. The aromatic qualities of cookies are integral to the overall enjoyment of these baked delights. As such, measures must be taken to safeguard these flavors from the clutches of external influences. Choosing containers with strong seals, avoiding storage alongside spicy foods, and opting for opaque containers to shield cookies from light all protect their aromatic integrity.

In conclusion, storing cookies for freshness is a multifaceted endeavor that demands attention to detail, understanding the variables at play, and a commitment to preserving the essence of these delectable treats. Each aspect contributes to the overarching goal of maintaining cookie quality over time, from the choice of containers and strategic use of moisture-retaining elements to temperature control, freezing techniques, and thoughtful packaging. As bakers and enthusiasts embark on this culinary journey, they not only extend the lifespan of their creations but also ensure that the joy and satisfaction derived from each delicious bite endure long after the final crumb has vanished.

Tips for Freezing and Shipping Holiday Treats

The holiday season brings abundant joy, warmth, and the aromatic delights of homemade treats. As friends and family gather, the exchange of festive goodies becomes a cherished tradition, transcending distances and connecting loved ones through the shared experience of holiday flavors. Yet, the logistics of preserving the freshness of these delectable creations can pose a challenge, especially when faced with the need to freeze and ship holiday treats. Navigating the delicate balance between preserving flavor and ensuring goodies arrive in perfect condition requires a strategic approach encompassing thoughtful freezing techniques and meticulous packaging for a seamless holiday treat exchange.

Freezing holiday treats is a practical solution for those who prefer to get a head start on their baking or for those intending to share the joy of homemade treats over an extended period. However, not all treats are created equal in the freezer's embrace. The type of treat and its ingredients play a significant role in determining the most suitable freezing approach. For cookies and bars, such as gingerbread cookies or peppermint brownies, freezing them in a single layer on a baking sheet before transferring them to an airtight container prevents them from sticking together. In contrast, more delicate treats, such as frosted cupcakes or cream-filled pastries, may benefit from being individually wrapped before freezing to safeguard their structural integrity and prevent frosting mishaps.

Timing also plays a crucial role in the freezing process. While the immediacy of freezing freshly baked treats might be tempting, allowing them to cool completely on a wire rack is a prerequisite. This cooling period ensures optimal texture and minimizes the risk of condensation, which could compromise the treat's quality during the freezing process. It's a delicate dance between sealing in the freshness and preventing the formation of ice crystals that might alter the treats' texture upon thawing.

As the freezer becomes a temporary haven for holiday delights, the choice of containers becomes paramount. Airtight containers with secure lids act as guardians against the invasion of unwanted freezer flavors and prevent treats from succumbing to freezer burn. Layering goodies with parchment paper or wax paper within the container provides an extra shield, preventing them from sticking together and preserving their individual qualities. Stacking treats space efficiently within the container and ensures that every inch of freezer real estate is utilized wisely.

The freezer's chilly embrace, however, is not an indefinite sanctuary. The optimal duration for freezing treats depends on the specific treat type and its ingredients. While cookies and bars can withstand several weeks in the freezer, other goodies, particularly those with high moisture content, such as cheesecakes or custard-filled pastries, may have a shorter lifespan. Consequently, meticulous labeling with the freezing date becomes a helpful guide, preventing the accidental oversight of long-forgotten treasures buried in the freezer depths.

Beyond the confines of the home kitchen, the challenge of sharing holiday treats becomes an exercise in ensuring that the season's delights traverse the miles unscathed. Shipping holiday treats demands careful planning and strategic packaging to guarantee that the recipients experience the same festive joy as if the treats were freshly baked. As a fundamental principle, the selection of goodies for shipping should lean toward those with a sturdy constitution—treats that can withstand the rigors of travel without sacrificing their visual appeal or flavor.

The packaging process begins with the choice of a suitable shipping container. Sturdy, corrugated cardboard boxes provide a protective outer layer, shielding threats from potential bumps and jostles during transit. Selecting a box size that accommodates treats comfortably without excessive empty space is imperative, minimizing the risk of movement within the box. This snug fit and appropriate cushioning ensure goodies arrive at their destination in the same pristine condition they embarked on on their journey.

The following line of defense consists of cushioning materials like crumpled newspaper, packing peanuts, or bubble wrap. Surrounding treats with a protective layer minimizes the risk of breakage and cushions them against external pressures. For delicate charms with intricate decorations, individual packaging in clear cellophane or plastic wrap adds an extra layer of protection, preventing them from losing their visual allure en route.

Temperature considerations come into play as treats embark on their shipping adventure. Optimal shipping times, particularly during cooler weather, reduce the risk of treats succumbing to the challenges of heat-induced melting. For treats with a perishable nature, such as cream-filled pastries, expedited shipping options may be a worthwhile investment to ensure their timely arrival while maintaining freshness.

The final step in the shipping process involves sealing the box with sturdy tape and reinforcing seams to prevent potential breaches during transit. A clear label indicating the contents and any specific handling instructions is a courteous guide for the journey ahead. Moreover, including a festive note or card adds a personal touch, turning to receive holiday treats into a heartwarming experience.

Throughout the freezing and shipping processes, communication emerges as a critical component. Whether freezing treats for personal enjoyment or shipping them to loved ones, sharing details about the treats' characteristics, optimal storage conditions, and any specific instructions for thawing or reheating ensures that the joy of the holiday treats extends beyond the act of consumption. This open dialogue fosters an appreciation for the effort invested in creating and preserving these delights, transforming the exchange of goodies into a shared celebration of holiday traditions.

In conclusion, the art of freezing and shipping holiday treats is a delicate dance that balances preserving flavors and textures with transportation logistics. From strategic freezing techniques that cater to the characteristics of each charm to meticulous packaging and temperature considerations during shipping, each step contributes to the seamless exchange of holiday delights. As the joy of homemade treats transcends physical distances, the careful execution of these processes ensures that the warmth and festivity of the holiday season are not confined to the kitchen but shared and celebrated with loved ones near and far.

CONCLUSION

As we reach the final chapter of "A Winter Magic Tour Through Holiday Cookies: Whisking Up Winter Magic – Introduction to Holiday Cookies," I extend heartfelt gratitude for joining us on this enchanting exploration of the sweetest season. The journey through these pages has celebrated tradition, creativity, and the magical moments that come alive in the heart of winter.

Our tour began with a nod to the essential ingredients and tools, guiding you through the basics of holiday cookie baking. From classic recipes that evoke nostalgia to inventive twists that spark inspiration, each chapter unfolded a new layer of the winter magic embedded in the art of crafting festive treats.

In the world of holiday cookies, we traversed international landscapes, discovering the rich tapestry of flavors that various cultures bring to their celebrations. We explored the realm of gluten-free and vegan options, ensuring that everyone can partake in the joy of baking during this particular season.

The journey didn't stop at baking alone; it extended to the art of decorating, hosting cookie swaps, and creating gifts that carry the warmth of homemade love. We encouraged you to document your winter magic, transforming family traditions into a personalized cookbook that preserves the essence of these moments for generations to come.

As the aroma of freshly baked cookies lingers in your home and the joy of sharing these delectable creations brightens your gatherings, we hope this e-book has inspired your baking endeavors and become a companion in creating lasting memories.

In the spirit of the holidays, let these cookies be more than a treat for the taste buds; let them symbolize the love, togetherness, and joy that define this magical season. From our kitchen to yours, may the warmth of these recipes continue to kindle the fires of festive cheer, making every winter day a celebration of sweet magic.

Thank you for whisking up winter magic with us. Happy baking, and may your holidays be filled with the sweetness that only a tray of freshly baked holiday cookies can bring!

Thank you for buying and reading/ listening to our book. If you found this book useful/ helpful please take a few minutes and leave a review on the platform where you purchased our book. Your feedback matters greatly to us.